INSIDE JOB

**TREATING MURDERERS
AND SEX OFFENDERS.
THE LIFE OF A PRISON
PSYCHOLOGIST.**

INSIDE
JOB

DR REBECCA MYERS

HARPER
element

HarperElement
An imprint of HarperCollins*Publishers*
1 London Bridge Street
London SE1 9GF

www.harpercollins.co.uk

HarperCollins*Publishers*
1st Floor, Watermarque Building, Ringsend Road
Dublin 4, Ireland

First published by HarperElement 2022

1 3 5 7 9 10 8 6 4 2

© Dr Rebecca Myers 2022

Dr Rebecca Myers asserts the moral right to
be identified as the author of this work

A catalogue record of this book is
available from the British Library

ISBN 978-0-00-853848-4

Printed and bound in the UK using 100%
renewable electricity at CPI Group (UK) Ltd

MIX
Paper | Supporting
responsible forestry
FSC™ C007454

This book is produced from independently certified FSC™ paper
to ensure responsible forest management.

For more information visit: www.harpercollins.co.uk/green

For the much-loved members of the
'Mayhem' WhatsApp group.

My safest place, and greatest adventure!

CONTENTS

Chapter One: Prison Virgin 1

Chapter Two: The Sex Offender Treatment
    Programme 16

Chapter Three: The Six Men 27

Chapter Four: A Group of My Own 37

Chapter Five: Sex Offender Treatment
    Programme in Action 47

Chapter Six: The Hot Seat 58

Chapter Seven: Trouble in the Group 68

Chapter Eight: Making Progress 76

Chapter Nine: The Professor and Victim Letters 92

Chapter Ten: Re-enacting the Offences 103

Chapter Eleven: Victim Empathy Role Plays 110

Chapter Twelve: Imposter Syndrome 117

Chapter Thirteen: Group End 132

Chapter Fourteen: Psychopath 144

Chapter Fifteen: The Extended Programme 157

Chapter Sixteen: Life Maps 168

Chapter Seventeen: Delving Deeper 180

Chapter Eighteen: There Is Something Wrong
with Me 197

Chapter Nineteen: We Are All Human 206

Chapter Twenty: Schemas 225

Chapter Twenty-One: Schema Modification 233

Chapter Twenty-Two: Attachment Styles 247

Chapter Twenty-Three: Sex and Relationships 255

Chapter Twenty-Four: Hostage 265

Chapter Twenty-Five: A Shift Inside 276

Chapter Twenty-Six: About Twenty Years Later 286

Epilogue 299

Acknowledgements 309

CHAPTER ONE

PRISON VIRGIN

My heart is thudding inside my chest like a trapped bird against glass. To my right is an enormous concrete wall capped with a metal tube and, balancing on top, a curling roll of razor wire. To my left is one of the red-brick wings of the maximum-security Graymoor prison, dotted with rows of tiny white barred windows. The cells. A low wolf-whistle and a shout cut through the drizzle. I cannot see where from, but someone can see me. A man with an Alsatian is patrolling the lonely strip of green at the bottom of the wall. The dog strains on his choker lead, pulling the prison officer along. Both dog and man have their eyes low, searching for contraband thrown over the wall.

We walk down the wide tarmac drag until we reach the arched wooden door of the old prison. I'm with my newly appointed supervisor, Louise, a senior forensic psychologist. She draws a bunch of oversized keys from the leather pouch on her belt and unlocks the door to reveal a barred gate. It swings heavily inwards to allow us to pass into what is known as the 'Centre' of the prison. I look up, not expecting the tall ceiling. It's a domed, circular space and radiating from it like spider's legs are four wings, four floors high, all encased in cream metal bars and steel mesh.

The first thing that strikes me is the distinctive smell. An institutional cocktail of unwashed, incarcerated men and boiled vegetables, brewed courtesy of the fusty air circulating through the Victorian prison's heating and ventilation system. The second thing is the noise. A loud, deep, constant mumble of men talking. No one voice identifiable, rather a current of sound, like a rumbling river. Occasionally there is a yell or a call, one voice rising above the flow. And doors banging. Metal on metal clanging. It is the unnerving sound of cell doors shutting.

I stand on the grey Centre floor trying to breathe, my mouth dry. It is like being ensnared in a large metal cage. From where I am standing, I can see through the barred gates of each wing and down the landings. Each floor is lined on both sides with rows of green metal doors. There are no windows, but the high white ceiling gives a strange illusion of freedom and space to the meshed enclosure I am standing in.

It is lunchtime and the prisoners are moving back to their cells after a morning in the workshops or education. Not shackled or handcuffed, just walking along like men leaving an office or factory at the end of a shift. An assorted collection of beings dressed in blue jeans and striped blue-and-white shirts. They look like normal men. Young and old, some black, some white, occasionally smart, mostly scruffy, but the prison clothes and the knowledge that they have all committed heinous crimes makes me feel intimidated and unsure where to look. I glance down at my smart, polished heels, my exposed legs in their thin tights. I wish I had not worn a skirt. My jacket has a belt that squeezes my young waist, and it has an enormous burnt-orange fur collar. It is like having a warm, itchy fox draped around my neck and I am sweating. I follow Louise's lead. She stands there quietly, letting them pass. Occasionally a prisoner speaks to her – 'Hi, Miss' – and she nods in response.

I am attracting long stares of curiosity and interest. I look around. Louise and I are the only women in sight. I am twenty-two years old. A slim, blonde psychology graduate. There are close to 800 men in this prison, and they are on the move. A heady combination of murderers, rapists and child molesters. It strikes me that if all 800 prisoners do want to try to escape at that very moment, there is little that the meagre number of staff patrolling the constant stream of prisoners can do. I feel vulnerable as I stand and watch, but there is no imminent uprising. They stream past me, finding their home wing, conditioned and toeing the line. To my utter relief, we move into the Centre office for safety.

The reprieve is temporary. Entering the Centre office is like entering the spider's lair. It is full of maybe a dozen male prison officers in officious blue-and-white uniform and shiny boots. I stand there in my new Topshop suit feeling overawed and eyeing the floor again, shrinking behind Louise. Feeling like a trapped fly, I am not sure where I am attracting the most unwanted attention: in the office with the male staff or standing outside with the murderers and rapists. Several of the officers stop what they are doing to look me up and down at leisure, taking in the only skirt in sight with undisguised pleasure. It is the late 1990s. Fresh-faced young females are as rare as hen's teeth in maximum-security prisons. Especially those bedecked in fur.

'What's this young lass doin' in 'ere? Is school out?' one mutters.

Another chuckles in response.

The Centre office is the hub of the prison and from its large glass windows the staff can see each wing and down along each landing, such is the design of the radial Victorian prisons. There are no corners to block the view, helping to keep staff and prisoners safe, and order and control in the jail. It is a busy spot. Several officers are watching 'line route' – the prisoners moving en masse around the jail under staff supervision. Staff come in and out, and the radios on their belts buzz and crackle like wasps. Clipboards with curling lists hang haphazardly on hooks at every available spot on the brick walls my response. I adopt Louise's approach and non-committal nod, as free from anxiety as I c Through the thin glass windows, I can see continuing to flow past, no more than a away. How and where would they g

At the time I had not given m safety. I rationalised that I with a prisoner, never one. Yet infamous was drawn to th programmes crime boo extraor som th

previous murder and cannibalism of a fellow patient in hospital, had killed two inmates, storing one of them under his bed. It brought his murder tally up to four.

'It's OK,' reassures the little PO. 'It's a long time ago. Bob lives in the Block now. For as long as I can remember. And probably as long as he can too,' he says with a chuckle.

He means the Segregation Block where prisoners are kept in isolation for either their own safety, or for the safety of others. I can see the other officers watching for

give a
an muster.
the prisoners
couple of metres
et a knife from?

ch thought to my physical
would not be left on my own
mind a dangerous or notorious
prisoners were part of the reason I
work. I was an avid spectator of TV
about prisons, and a consumer of real-life
ks. Such crimes attract public attention in
dinary degrees and the more macabre and grue-
e the better, it seems. People want the gory details,
ne inside story. I wasn't after the grisly details. I wanted
to try to understand why some humans make such terrible decisions and commit atrocious acts with appalling
consequences for themselves and others. I couldn't think
of anything more interesting or worthwhile to invest my
life in. I was also drawn in by a – somewhat voyeuristic
– altruism and I was desperate to meet and talk to these
strange, hidden and caged creatures and see how they
were different from the rest of us.

Throughout my degree I was set on this being my
career and I knew exactly where I wanted to be: a maximum-security prison for men. I never had any real
interest in working with women. Women seemed too

complex, tragic and emotional. Men seemed far simpler. Perhaps I veered away from trying to fathom women because of my complicated relationship with my own mother. She left the family home – me, my father and two younger sisters – when I was about fourteen years old after having an affair. My sister tells me we came home from school one day and she had gone. Bolted. We were abandoned. Three eggs left in a nest before we had fledged.

I don't really remember it. I think I put the rejection and the loss to one side and then got on with being as rebellious, self-indulgent and irresponsible as I could – including collecting petty criminal, fixer-upper boyfriends – all in a self-destructive attempt at attention seeking. My dependable, devoted father picked up the pieces.

As soon as I could I was off travelling and then to London and university for more pleasure-seeking, but with bells on, as the house music and rave scene took off in the early 1990s. Dressed in the tiniest, shiniest of outfits picked up from the haze of Camden Market, I indulged in the various stimulants on offer so I could dance for ten hours straight in huge, thumping ware-houses with dripping-wet walls. Weekends were a hedonistic escape that left no room in my head for anything but the reassuring beat of the music. I succumbed to a tattoo here, several piercings there (perhaps my form of self-harm), all of which had to be later removed or kept covered for my new law-abiding and respectful job in the prison service. A world away from that coveted spot in front of the speakers.

At least two of my previous boyfriends ended up in prison. One memorable unsuitable had a glass eye to replace the real one lost in a shooting accident, a pit bull and an array of Union Jack tattoos. Fresh out of prison and the local hard man, he was well known to all, and there was an inherent status in being his girlfriend. I wonder if I was drawn to trying to repair challenging men. Maybe it was a distraction for avoiding mending myself. Maybe those who have been through some form of trauma are drawn to the psychologically damaged. Working at HMP Graymoor was certainly going to offer the ultimate challenge in fixer-uppers.

Later that first week, before I am to be given keys, I am instructed to attend 'the Security Talk'. I trot off down the corridor of the admin block and find myself in a small, cluttered room with three prison officers squeezed in around untidy desks. One of them is extremely hand-some and not much older than me. He has chestnut hair, caramel skin and chocolate eyes, all of which are enhanced by the uniform. He smiles at me, and I notice his perfect teeth.

'You must be Rebecca. I'm Dominic.'

I feel myself blushing, redness rising slowly like a sunrise up my neck and bursting onto my cheeks. One of the other officers has spotted it like an apex predator would its prey.

'Bloody hell, you're in there, Dom. Look at the colour of that lass's cheeks!'

'Let's get down to business,' he says, grinning.

'Easy, lad!' chortles the officer. He looks like an egg with his bald head and shiny, hairless face.

'Come on, away from these idiots,' Dominic offers. He gives me a quick wink as the officer does a pumping action with his arm.

With my personal sunrise still glowing, I am glad to be out of their den. Dominic spends the morning with me, covering security basics including what you cannot bring into the prison – umbrellas and metal cutlery (potential weapons), chewing gum and Blu Tack (useful for blocking up keyholes and can also be used by prisoners for imprinting and then copying keys). There is a strict dress code, which includes not wearing scarves or necklaces (strangulation risk) or anything revealing. No high heels in case you must run. He doesn't mention fur, but I have already struck that one off my list. He talks to me about grooming and manipulation. How prisoners can build up powerful relationships over time with staff, then encourage them to start bringing in, or taking out, prohibited items, make mistakes or do favours.

It is time for a visit to 'The Black Museum', as Dominic calls it, a dusty glass cabinet in the corridor full of illicit items made or obtained by prisoners. I peer in.

Dominic is standing behind me and is clearly looking at my bottom. There are several rusty razor blades moulded onto toothbrushes. The really lethal ones have two razor blades side by side instead of bristles, so if slashed with this the medics cannot easily sew you back together. I see huge, ugly knives handmade from plastic, metal or glass, and tiny, deadly shanks with grubby string around the handle so they can be held without injuring the perpetrator. Time, ingenuity and improvisation are all that is needed, it seems. I now know where Maudsley got his knife. There is even an attempt at a gun. Dominic proudly assures me it has a working mechanism. I consider the assorted collection of offensive weapons and escape tools. Is the sole purpose of the museum to terrify new staff?

Dominic also gives me 'The Key Talk'. I cannot believe that they are going to give me a set of keys to a maximum-security prison and trust me to walk around with them *and* lock every door behind me. I struggle to remember to switch my hair straighteners off at home. I silently pray I won't be the one to drop the ball. Imagine being responsible for an escape. I know I will worry about the keys endlessly.

'Get a room, you two!' shouts the egg-headed officer as we leave to visit the Segregation Block.

* * *

In the Block a gang of male staff are sitting about drinking tea, no doubt ready for action and waiting for feeding time like keepers at a zoo. They look up at me like I am a new exhibit. The officer in charge is female. The only woman I have met outside of the sterile admin area so far, and to my relief she offers to show me round. As we descend the metal steps into the Block's concrete bowels, I can see the line of cells down one side, each housing one human. It reminds me of a rehoming centre for unwanted dogs. We are underground and the artificial lights bounce off the white walls and shining grey floor. I cannot see any prisoners.

We walk along the row of cells. A pair of lace-free prison-issue pumps sit outside each one, waiting for their owner. The metal doors have a small observation flap, and a furtive, dark pupil appears at one as we pass. A prisoner presses his searching black eyeball against the glass. I am not sure which one of us is on display. I turn away first.

'And that's Maudsley,' says the officer, pointing to an unusual cell.

Maudsley has a fish-tank-like cubicle, different from the other cells. We can glance in and he can glare out. It is like observing a creature in a waterless aquarium, perhaps a rare captive shark. Maudsley looks up. A pale, scrawny man with grey straggly hair. Maudsley is the first man to receive a whole life tariff (meaning he will never be reviewed for release by the Parole Board) after the murder of the two prisoners at HMP Graymoor. He is destined to live and die in that sparse, subterranean glass cage beneath the prison. I wonder what he does all day. Poetry, according to my impatient guide.

'We've also got Bronson,' she says, nodding to another cell.

I have heard of Charles Bronson. He is one of the most violent and revered prisoners in the system. I am tempted but dare not look at their most famous inmate for fear he might speak to me, and I won't have a clue what to say.

'Charlie likes to take staff hostage and can't be managed on normal location. But I get on with him really well,' she adds.

How does she achieve this? How do you 'get on well' with the most hostile and menacing prisoners in the system? I wonder. I'm worried I won't be able to handle the officers, never mind the prisoners.

My tour of the Segregation Block over, Dominic now takes me to visit the wings. We step into the wing office on Bravo Wing. It's a cramped, dingy room in the middle of the 'Two's' (ground floor) landing where the staff hang out, overseeing the safety and running of the wing. The obligatory clipboards with lists of surnames and prison numbers hang off the walls. First names are redundant here. I spot a Page Three calendar on the wall with NSPCC stickers over the model's breasts. Dominic introduces me to the wing senior officer (SO) on duty.

'This is Rebecca, our brand-new psychologist. She's come to sort us all out!'

The wing SO, a tall, gaunt man with crater-like acne scars, nods in my direction and ogles my chest. I pull my jacket across my breasts.

A plump, sweaty officer with wispy hair like an over-ripe dandelion is wedged in at the desk reading a red-topped newspaper. I look at him and wonder how he will extract himself and run if there is an emergency on the wing. He sighs an exasperated sigh.

'More bloody do-gooders. Waste of time. These cons just need a good hangin'. And what's with all these chicks in here nowadays, Dom? Bloody liability if you ask me,' he grumbles, without lifting his eyes from the paper and taking a satisfying slurp of his tea.

Dominic smiles but does not answer. I turn a blind eye to the calendar with the stickered breasts, the chauvinistic, sexist attitudes and behaviour. I am overwhelmed and outnumbered. I am not standing up for human rights, feminism or equality, though, and I feel a distinct lack of girl power.

I get to know the small but expanding Psychology Department. Louise is my gentle, intensely feminist supervisor. I wonder why on earth she chose to work in Graymoor. Alex Bull is a newly qualified psychologist. She is a conspicuous, bouncy, red-headed Scot, who likes to talk about herself and her military career and smokes a lot. Bronwyn, another trainee like me, is warm and witty and quickly becomes my confidante and partner in crime. The head of the department is a petite, armour-plated blonde called Maxine, who is never seen without full make-up, sticky fuchsia lip gloss and a perfect mani-cure. She can spot a transgression by a trainee at a thousand paces.

'Max – sharper than an axe, that woman,' says Bronwyn with delight one day. So, Max/Axe becomes 'The Axe Murderer' and we watch each other's backs like hawks.

The role of the psychologists in the prison is to interview the prisoners and write risk assessments for the Parole Board, deliver programmes and carry out psychological assessments. I have been employed on the basis that I will be delivering the newly introduced programmes. The prisoners at Graymoor are some of the most devi-ant, dangerous and highest-risk violent and sexual offenders in the system. As a brand-new graduate, fresh from working in and dancing on bars in Greece for the summer, I have little idea as to what this is going to entail.

I have been allocated a cell in the old hospital block where the Psychology Department is housed. My new office has a barred window looking out onto the prisoner exercise yard where the uniformed men circle twice a day, smoking and chatting. The heating system is a painted, chipped pipe that runs along the bottom of the wall. I am told it will not be switched on until there is ice on the inside of the window. An internal door leads to an old, stained metal toilet and sink with cold running water. An en-suite. I smoke in the office to add a little ambience. Incredibly, I have a name plaque on the door, with the title 'Trainee Psychologist'.

CHAPTER TWO

THE SEX OFFENDER TREATMENT PROGRAMME

The mid–late 1990s sees the beginning of a tsunami of cognitive behavioural therapy (CBT) programmes rolled out across Her Majesty's Prison Service, England and Wales, including stress management, violence reduction, thinking skills and the Sex Offender Treatment Programme (SOTP). The premise of all these CBT programmes is that if you can change thinking, you can change behaviour.

The SOTP started in 1992 and is a manualised group work programme of eighty to ninety sessions (approximately 180 hours) of intensive treatment delivered by a team of three trained, multi-disciplinary facilitators – psychologists, prison and probation officers, and occasionally education and chaplaincy staff. Research into men who commit sexual offences, and their treatment, has been growing since the 1960s and the HM Prison Service SOTP is considered an international leader in the field. Although the initial premise was borrowed from Canada, nowhere else in the world is there a coordinated, research-driven roll-out of manual-ised programmes across multiple prison sites. A long-term evaluation of its effectiveness will be critical, yet it is pending, as in the 1990s we are still in the early years of treatment. In terms of the SOTP it is very much the underlying principle that sex offenders cannot be cured, but they can learn to recognise and manage their harmful thinking and behaviour. They can learn to stop offending if they are motivated to do so but must prac-tise the skills for the rest of their lives.

I quickly become involved in the assessment of sexual offenders for the SOTP groups, including prisoners who have committed rape, child abuse and sexual murder. The psychologists and assistants complete these assess-ments one to one. They involve taking a personal history, including sexual behaviours and preferences, document-ing the extent and type of the sexual offending, checking that the prisoner is not in total denial and whether he is willing to talk about his motivations and offences in a forthcoming group. Around 50 per cent of the prisoners we approach deny their offences, either outright (they were not there/wrongly convicted) or partially ('we had sex, but it was consensual' or 'it only happened once').

I shadow a few SOTP assessments with one of the psychology assistants and then am encouraged to fly solo. I am terrified. I don't feel ready. It will just be the sex offender and me, on our own in the wing interview room, which is a prison cell where the bed has been taken out and replaced with a desk.

I head up to the wing feeling almost as nervous about going into the wing office as meeting the sex offender. It is the luck of the draw as to how intimidating it will be, and how amenable the staff will be with regards to helping. I have tried to ingratiate myself with them at every opportunity, moulding to what they need me to be, like a social chameleon. This means being pleasant, cheerful and oozing humility, but not being too keen. It means a degree of shrewd flirting in order to gain a little influence and make them willing to assist me. I hide my womanliness under my clothes yet need to use it in my favour. It is my hidden power and I work on it every single day.

I get a good ignoring as I enter the wing staff hide. I offer a Marlboro Light, laugh at an inappropriate joke about a female colleague, slip into a broader accent than my middle-class upbringing dictates and ask for the prisoner. One of the seated officers leans forward, slides the glass window across and hollers down the wing, 'JONES 157. PSYCHO CALL-UP!'

Eventually my first 'call-up' potters down the wing to meet me, all four and a half scruffy feet of him. His face is creased with age and he looks like he needs a good iron. He is missing his teeth and one finger, and the remaining digits are earwax yellow from nicotine. He smells of a filth I can't place – a mixture of sweat, smoke and a rotting kitchen bin. I lead him to the interview room and try to remember the correct security protocol in the office, seating him away from the door so I can get out if I need to. I check that the newly issued rape alarm is accessible but is not going to go off by accident, prompting a stampede of officers. I note the position of the alarm box on the wall that will summon the staff, hopefully – I dare not test it. And here I am. Totally alone in a cell with a convicted sex offender who is free to do what he wants. There is no officer. No handcuffs. No radio. Only the grubby little man across the desk and me. He looks more petrified than I do.

I run through the paperwork, asking him about his convictions against two female children. He mumbles his answers and blames the victims. 'They came onto me. They were wearing revealing clothes. They sat on my knee, took their clothes off. They liked it. They asked for more. They didn't tell anyone. My wife knew and didn't say anything.' The girls were his daughters, aged six and ten, and he raped them, repeatedly. I have no idea what to say, so I just write it down, business like, and concentrate on asking the questions. I have to ask him about his sex life and if he has ever been abused. If he has ever had sex with animals. It's embarrassing to be asking these questions of a man. A stranger. A child rapist. He can't look at me and focuses on rolling ciga-rette after cigarette, licking the papers with his quick, wet tongue. I find it repulsive and can't look at him. We are both glad when it's over and he scurries out of the room and back to his cell without looking back. I wasn't scared of him, and I survived it, but I feel overcome with how little I know and how much I have to learn.

I do several SOTP assessments over the first few months and start to see patterns in what the prisoners tell me: the ongoing denial; the constant blaming of the victims, drugs and alcohol, or the circumstances. There always seems to be a reason and a justification for their behaviour. Some excuses are ridiculous.

'Someone must have come along and raped the body after I killed her. It definitely wasn't me and I did leave her in a public place.' (A hedge.)

'We were in the lift, and I must have had a fit. When I came around my trousers were by my knees, and it had happened.'

'I slipped and my penis just ended up there by accident.'

'I must have a missing twin.' (In response to DNA being left at the scene.)

Even in the face of these incredible statements, the prisoners stand fast, roll out the excuses and appear as if they have come to believe them. I think in some cases they have. Who would want to admit to these appalling acts? Most of the prisoners explain away the abuse or rape as consensual, even when the children were very young or weapons were used. Many of them seem ashamed to talk to me, skipping over bits of the story, leaving gaping holes and avoiding the details. What stands out is that every single man I speak to is convinced he will never do it again. I am not sure how to deal with this to start with, although with practice I learn that an effective challenge is something like: 'Had I asked you before your current offence if you would do it, what might you have said?' Invariably the prisoners reply that they could not have predicted it, and then there is dissonance, a chink of wiggle room for a discussion about how, perhaps, future behaviour cannot be predicted either.

It feels like an honour to be part of the developing SOTP, and after doing a handful of SOTP assessments, I am asked to attend the national SOTP training to become a facilitator for the treatment sessions. Graymoor is crammed with sexual offenders and is a leading treatment centre with several groups running at one time. I don't know what happens in the eighty-plus treatment sessions that take place in a draughty room on the prison wing. It all feels a bit secretive. I hear a rumour that they role play the offences, acting out rape and murder. I can't believe that this is true and am apprehensive as I head off to the training.

The training is held at the Prison Service College, a grand eighteenth-century country house with stone turrets. It has previously been used to train spies during the Second World War. The two formidable ladies at Reception look like they have been working here since the Spitfires roared overhead, and the rudimentary accommodation, icy communal bathrooms and institutionalised beige food offerings continue the theme. Perhaps fifty nervous psychologists, prison and probation officers gather to learn the ropes.

One of the first things we cover is effective treatment style and the impact a facilitator has on a group. Elizabeth, the lead trainer and a glamorous Princess Diana lookalike, explains that facilitators need to be warm, open, approachable and responsive, but also to mix in the perfect amount of challenge. Cold, punitive styles are not helpful and are, in fact, known to be damaging to the therapeutic process. Any facilitator undertaking the SOTP who does not have the appropriate therapeutic style will not pass the course, she clarifies with a warm, wide smile in a perfect pink shade of Clinique.

The training covers theories of sexual offending and the concept of the decision chain. Based on the cognitive-behavioural approach (that thinking underpins behaviour), the decision-chain exercise consists of identifying the key situations, thoughts, feelings and behaviour that led to the offence. In theory it allows the offenders to understand the build-up to their offence and identify the triggers for it.

And the rumours are true. We *will* be re-enacting rape, murder and child abuse via the victim empathy role plays. By getting the men to play their victim, the aim is to allow them to experience the victim's perspective of the offending, supposedly allowing emotional empathy to develop, and therefore preventing future offences. A specialist trainer with a background in acting is brought in and, despite my fears, her confidence and professionalism inspire and reassure me. She and Elizabeth – who is as intelligent as she is beautiful – make it look simple. A role player dressed as a prisoner allows us to practise. He is so true to life that I am almost convinced he is an escapee.

Ethically, I can see that the role plays may be controversial and that the rules of safety and boundaries will have to be followed. In the groups the prisoners are to be allowed a 'time-out' at any stage. Any physical touching is to be limited and agreed beforehand. At no point will there be any intimate touching. Props, such as pens, can be used to simulate weapons or the offender's penis or fingers. It feels like an immense responsibility with a potential to end in utter disaster. It becomes clearer why a punitive style is not appropriate, yet I cannot imagine doing this with real rapists and child molesters. How will it ever work? How will they agree? How will we stop the rest of the group laughing or sabotaging it? As a young woman, how will I rhythmically poke a pretend penis into a convicted rapist's leg in a room full of sex offenders to simulate rape?

These re-enactments are already running in prisons across the country and receiving favourable responses. Prisoners are saying that the role-plays are life-changing and will stop them offending in the future. I trust the inspirational Elizabeth, the dedicated SOTP team and knowledgeable trainers. We are the flagship and leading the way on the international stage with our treatment programmes. I think we all just want to make a difference and put ourselves out of a job, whatever it takes.

We are also introduced to the notion of cognitive distortions (CDs). These are excuses that allow someone to justify their own behaviour.

'We all do it,' says Elizabeth. 'Give ourselves little excuses in our heads to justify our actions. For example, eating cake, I say to myself, "It's only a little piece, it won't do any harm." Offenders make these excuses too.'

These CDs are to be challenged through a process known as Socratic questioning. This is an approach which uses open questions, rather than closed questions (i.e. those that prompt yes/no answers), to help the offender start to consider his thinking differently. The questioning of the offender's thinking is to be carried out in a 'spirit of genuine inquiry', which aims to help the offender reach his own answers. It is thought that people are more likely to internalise learning if they discover it themselves, rather than being lectured by others.

* * *

It is an exhausting two weeks and on the final night I am sitting with John, the role player. He is far less terrifying in real life – a cheery, bearded man who chuckles his way through the evening and several pints. He tells me a story about how in the last hotel he ran the training in, he recognised a group of people from a previous course and went over to ask them how their SOTP groups were running. They eyed him like he was an extra-terrestrial, so he expanded a little more and introduced himself as 'John, the sex offender role player'. As he was talking it dawned on him why they were familiar … they were not sex offender therapists, but the cast of *Emmerdale*.

I scan the room at the clusters of people gathered on the faded leather sofas, chatting, drinking and laughing. We have become a close group, brought together by an unusual shared experience, and they feel like my tribe. Some people have become particularly intimate and the nocturnal visits down the corridors are not all about using the communal toilets. We have lived and breathed this course, spotting our own 'CDs' constantly. 'CD!' we call out in unison if someone is justifying another pudding or trip to the bar. No doubt the night-time antics are justified too. There are serious conversations about how challenging the work will be and whether we will be able to do it for real, but few about how we may cope or the potential effects it might have on us.

I am sorry the two weeks have come to an end. I have met some wonderful, committed, caring people who sincerely want to make a difference in the world, and I have a serious professional crush on Elizabeth. I am scared, petrified even, at the thought of running an SOTP group, but also naively enthused at the thought of delving further into why some men commit such atrocious sexual offences and murder. I want to see, hear and explore it for myself and not just read it out of one of my true-crime books. And my first SOTP group of six sexual offenders is already selected and waiting for me back at Graymoor.

CHAPTER THREE

THE SIX MEN

Jeremy is convicted of kidnap, rape and murder and has received two life sentences, with a tariff of twenty-five years. Often written as ninety-nine years in prison files, a life sentence does mean an offender is sentenced to be in custody for the rest of his life. However, the sentencing judge gives a tariff, the minimum term an offender must spend in prison before becoming eligible for parole. The Parole Board must then decide whether a prisoner meets the test for release; that is, does the offender need to be confined in custody for the protection of the public? If they do not meet the test, then they must remain in custody until their next parole board – usually two to three years – when the process begins again and continues for the rest of his natural life.

Jeremy was a serving police officer and as such had no criminal history. He had kidnapped his forty-five-year-old female neighbour at gunpoint and taken her to a secluded spot where he raped her. A local man walking his dog interrupted them and Jeremy shot him in the face and then shot the dog. Both died at the scene. He then threatened to kill the victim and himself. The victim talked him out of it and encouraged him to take her home. Jeremy drove himself to his own police station and handed himself in, giving them his gun, clothes and shoes in sealed bags for evidence. He was thirty-four years old.

Jeremy is now forty-five years old. His behaviour in prison has been exemplary and he has kept himself busy by starting an Open University degree and working in the prison library. He likes to put in the occasional complaint about the rules or the staff not doing things properly. When assessed for the SOTP, he admitted to the offences but says he has no idea why they happened. There is very little else about him in the file. No criminal history, one devastating offence, and then no violence or rule-breaking since.

Nigel has also been convicted of murder. Like Jeremy, he received a mandatory life sentence – the only sentence a judge can hand down for murder. His victim was a thirteen-year-old schoolgirl. A married man and the father of a young son, Nigel had been a caretaker at some swimming baths and got to know the victim and her friend. One day the victim stayed behind after her swimming lesson and visited Nigel in the boiler room. He sexually assaulted her and then strangled her. He hid the body in the boiler room and went home to have tea with his wife and child. When he was arrested, the police found a large collection of children's underwear and pornography hidden in a locker in the boiler room. He did not admit the offence straight away, but in the face of much forensic evidence he accepted his guilt. He was twenty-nine years old.

It has taken five attempts to persuade him to do the SOTP and he is now in his mid-forties. He is terrified of the other prisoners finding out about his offence. Child killers do tough sentences. There is a distinct hierarchy in prisons, even among the most serious offences. Armed robbers are at the top of the ladder, followed by 'straight' murderers (non-sexual), and sexual offenders and/or murderers of the very elderly or young children on the bottom rung. Those lurking at the bottom of the pile must be careful, even in a prison like Graymoor – known as Monster Mansion – where about 80 per cent are sexual offenders. Although rare, attacks by other offenders do happen: sugar in boiling water thrown at the face or genitals to dissolve the skin, stabbings, contamination of the food by saliva, faeces or urine, and the very occasional murder.

Wayne received a discretionary life sentence (handed down for serious offences like rape or armed robbery) for five counts of rape. He has a long history of acquisitive offending (offences where you acquire something illegally) and driving and drugs offences, starting when he was thirteen years old. He racked up sixty-seven offences by the time he was handed life aged twenty-seven. He has two sexual pre-convictions. One is for indecent exposure. He exposed his penis to a woman on a bus when he was seventeen and received a community order. He has another pre-conviction for assault and indecent assault against a fifty-year-old woman when he was aged twenty. The victim was his mother.

Wayne committed a series of rapes on women in their own homes at night. He broke in wearing a gorilla mask and raped each woman in her own bed. This spree took place over three years. In the later rapes he took a knife. He also cut the phone wires and sometimes smashed the light bulbs. There was an intensive police hunt for a serial rapist, and he managed to evade capture for some time. He denied all the offences until the trial, where he pleaded guilty.

Now aged twenty-nine, Wayne has continued to take drugs in prison and has several adjudications (a formal hearing when there is an allegation that the prison rules have been broken; if found guilty there is a punishment) for having a positive drug test. He has twice been caught exposing his penis to female night staff. He denies that this was purposeful and states he was 'just sleeping with the covers off'. Wayne is under the care of a psychiatrist for anxiety and depression and is regularly on suicide watch. He attempted to hang himself at sentence and again last year. Staff frequently stop him from self-harming, and he has had numerous trips to an outside hospital to remove pieces of plastic, pens, paperclips and other debris from his arms and legs.

In the SOTP assessment he admitted to the rapes but was a closed book about his history. He stated that he wants to find out why he committed the offences and to make sure that he never does it again. He declared he would rather die in prison than commit another offence. He thought he would probably die in prison anyway, but that death would be the easy option.

Kyle also received discretionary life and has a six-year tariff for the rape and buggery of an eighteen-year-old female stranger. He had been out drinking with friends on Christmas Eve and met the victim in a nightclub, where he bought her several drinks and gave her some of his cocaine. CCTV caught him and two friends following her out of the club and talking to her outside. She then left without them. Kyle and his co-defendants followed her and dragged her into a graveyard, where they assaulted her. Kyle smashed her head on the wall and then they all raped her orally, vaginally and anally. Kyle used a condom. He stamped on her head before they left, fracturing her cheekbone and breaking her nose, urinated on her, ripped off all her clothes and dumped them in a skip on the way home, leaving the victim for dead.

Due to the CCTV footage, he was arrested quickly but vehemently denied any involvement in the offence, blaming his co-defendants. The case went to trial where the victim had to give evidence. The judge commented on his total lack of remorse and callousness. Despite his young age (twenty-two at sentence), Kyle has several pre-convictions, including grievous bodily harm (GBH) for breaking a taxi driver's jaw, robbery of handbags from women on the street, drugs, theft, breach of bail, escape from custody and a conviction for cruelty – shooting his dog with an air rifle. He had two children by different women when he was aged fifteen and seventeen and has met neither child.

Now twenty-six years old, Kyle has an extensive volatile prison history. He has been involved in assaults, the stabbing of another prisoner, disobeying lawful orders, dealing drugs, possession of hooch and bullying. He is frequently removed to the Segregation Block for fighting.

Kyle has undertaken a Psychopathy Check List-Revised (PCL-R) as part of the SOTP assessment. Psychopathy is a mental disorder, thought to be an extreme form of anti-social personality disorder. The Psychopathy Check List, developed by Dr Robert Hare, is the most widely used tool for assessing the presence – or absence – of traits associated with psychopathy. Traits include a callous lack of empathy, versatile criminal behaviour, shallow affect (i.e. not feeling or showing emotion even in very emotional situations) and impulsivity. The clinical cut-off for psychopathy used in the UK is twenty-five – out of forty – on the PCL-R. Kyle's score is thirty. The policy is to only accept one to two men above the cut-off on a group. This is due to high-scorers having the potential to cause disruption to the group work process, and the research that suggests psychopaths are notoriously difficult to treat. It is thought that the facilitators can only handle one to two psychopaths at once.

Frank is serving life for murder with a sixteen-year tariff. He murdered a female prostitute by strangulation in his car following sexual intercourse. He then took her body back to his girlfriend's house – who was away for the weekend – borrowed a shovel from the next-door neighbour and buried the victim in the garden. He tried to destroy the forensic evidence by burning her clothes and cleaning the car with bleach. He then hung quilts at the windows to block out any tell-tale light and waited for the police to arrive.

Frank is not convicted of a sexual offence; however, all men coming into Graymoor have their files analysed by the Psychology Department in order to consider if there is any sexual element to their offending. If the initial check reveals concerns, they are put forward for assessment for the SOTP. I had done the file review on Frank.

From my reading of the file, the sex was not consensual. Louise and I had talked through the signs to watch out for: bruising in certain areas – thighs, neck, breasts, vagina, anus; internal injuries; damage to (bites, cuts) or exposure of the sexual organs; disturbed clothing; cut, ripped or removed underwear; the presence of semen and the removal of nipples or pubic hair. The pathologist report was grim and challenging to read, yet it was professional, clinical and factual. It removed the emotion and became more like a puzzle I had to solve. I thought there was evidence that the sex was rape, even though Frank had not been convicted of it. I learnt that this can quite often be the case with murder when there has been a sexual element, as the offender will get a mandatory life sentence handed down for the murder alone.

Tucked away at the back of Frank's file was a tatty envelope. I opened it and out slid several colourful photographs of a suburban garden, complete with plastic garden furniture and child's slide. A naked, dark-haired, greenish-white-skinned woman was lying face down in a muddy ditch in the middle of the lawn, soil covering her legs. The image burned itself into my brain like a laser. Forever indelible. A brain tattoo. It was the lack of respect that got to me. I had worked in nursing homes for the elderly and demented. I had seen dead bodies. I had laid them out. I had washed the dead on their own beds, dressing them in clean nightwear and closing their vacant eyes. There had been no respect given here. She was dumped. Soil lumped on her. It was in her hair. She had been left to rot with no ceremony, no clothes and no one to shut her eyes. There were more graphic photos and close-ups of her damaged, purple neck. It felt intrusive to be looking. I returned the photos and some respect to the dead woman, putting her away from prying eyes and back into the unmarked brown envelope.

At the SOTP assessment, which I also did with Frank, he admitted to the murder. He also said he knew the sex was a 'bit rough' but was keen to point out that he had not been convicted of rape. He agreed to do the SOTP to explore what happened.

Andy's index offence (in other words his main, current offence) was the murder of a man. He had been part of a group who had beaten a man to death with a baseball bat over a drug debt. He received a life sentence with a thirteen-year tariff for his role in the offence. He has a history of violence: an actual bodily harm (ABH) and GBH, both against men, and several drugs offences. He also has a pre-conviction for two counts of indecent assault against his brother's female children (aged eight and ten at the time). These offences happened around ten years prior to the murder. However, given that they are part of his pattern of offending behaviour, as a life-sentenced prisoner he will be expected to address all areas of risk before being deemed suitable for release by the Parole Board.

Andy has served twelve years of his life sentence and has denied the indecent assaults the whole way through.

He has completed work on his use of violence. Now, as his parole window approaches, he has begrudgingly agreed to undertake the SOTP. At the SOTP assessment he admitted to touching the older victim on one occasion and said he will talk about this in treatment. During his time in prison, he has received a few adjudications for breaking the prison rules and getting into a couple of fights early on in his sentence, but nothing of recent concern. He is a red band (a trusted prisoner) and a wing cleaner – one of the most coveted prison jobs, which means he is allowed access to certain staffed areas of the jail that other prisoners are not, has more freedom on the wing and more time unlocked. He has agreed to do the SOTP on the basis that no one on the wing will find out about his sexual offences. He does not want his good reputation ruined.

So, this is my first group. I am twenty-three years old, with an undergraduate psychology degree and two weeks of SOTP training under my belt, and according to the wing staff I am 'still wet behind the ears'. For the next nine months I will be responsible for the treatment of six life-sentenced male sexual offenders, three of whom are Category A (assessed as the highest risk): Jeremy, Kyle and Frank. Four of them have committed murder. One is a notorious serial rapist, one a child killer and one a high-scoring psychopath. I am about to meet them all for the very first time.

CHAPTER FOUR

A GROUP OF MY OWN

I am sitting in one of the SOTP group rooms – a stale, circular place with peeling white paint. It is located just off the Centre and sandwiched between two wings. I can hear the usual noise of the jail outside. The clanging metal gates. The odd shout. The room has eight men in it. And me. We are sitting in a circle on tired upholstered prison chairs.

Two of the men are my co-facilitators. Daniel is a blue-eyed, shaven-headed prison officer in his early thirties. Strong, smooth arms with a couple of elaborate tattoos poke out from his pressed short-sleeved white shirt. He gives me a cheeky grin and a wink. Len, also an officer, is a hefty Yorkshireman with a thick accent, a crooked nose, gnawed fingernails and a lifetime of public service. After years in the army, he had been a Queen's Guard at Buckingham Palace prior to joining the prison service. He is chewing his nails and studying his SOTP manual. I'll run each following session with just one of the officers, but all three of us are here today, for the first day. The other six men are the sexual offenders. My palms are sweaty as I grip my own manual and pretend I am not reading it. The late-spring morning sunshine pokes through the windows that sit along one curved side of the room, creating a series of lines across the dirty, thin carpet from the shadows of the bars. It is already stuffy, and I can smell the sweat of the men. Outside I can see the wing and the rows of little white windows. Several cartons of milk are balanced outside on the windowsills for hope of keeping them fresh. As usual there are several nodding pigeons perched on the sills too, scrounging for scraps of food.

'Welcome to the group,' says Daniel, standing up. 'We'll be your SOTP tutors, and we'll meet in this room four times a week for the next nine or ten months. We are going to try to help you understand why you committed your offences and try to stop you from doing it again.'

The six men sit in silence, as if Daniel has just told them they are going to be buried alive.

'Now, we are going to go around the room and introduce ourselves. Please can you say briefly what your offence is too,' he says, sitting back down in his seat by the flip-chart board and its blank paper.

I remember what the SOTP trainers said. Would you want to talk about your most embarrassing secret in a room full of strangers? The men continue in their silence, although a couple reach for their tobacco tins and start to roll furiously. I speak. Trying to hide any waver in my voice and hoping that they will not notice. Praying that speaking in a group will not give me the familiar pink flush that I still struggle with when the attention is on me. I flushed red every time the register was called at school and I had to answer to my name. Today in the group room I have worn a high polo neck in preparation. It is inappropriate for the weather, but I cannot risk it. My legs are encased in familiar 'prison grey' loose trousers, now my usual safe attire.

'Who wants to go first? Don't worry, we are not writing this down. It's only saying hello, getting it out in the open,' I say.

Not too much of a tremble, flush held at bay under the polo neck. I am doing OK. Daniel catches my eye and smiles. In turn, I smile at the men, leaning my head to one side to demonstrate the 'spirit of genuine inquiry', just like Elizabeth taught me in training.

A slim man with insipid blue eyes, pallid skin under heavy attack from freckles, a shock of hair the colour of a tangerine and a pronounced cowlick, resulting in the hair growing at different angles in the centre of his forehead, speaks first.

'Er, hello, everyone.' He puts his equally freckly hand up in an awkward little wave and straightens his back. 'I am Jeremy. I am forty-five years old. I am – was, I mean … a police officer.'

There is a grunt from a well-built young man with heavy-looking dreadlocks, curled like snakes into a wide ponytail, to my right. Hearing it, Jeremy pauses and looks down at his pressed jeans. I notice that there is a crease ironed down the front, as if they are suit trousers. He has stopped talking.

'We need to have respect for each other or else this group is not going to work. What is your offence, Jeremy? Just a brief outline so it's out in the open,' says Daniel.

Jeremy swallows, his big hands gripping his knees. 'I kidnapped a woman and raped her, and when someone tried to rescue her, I killed him.'

Again, there is total silence in the room. Jeremy doesn't move a muscle.

'Thank you for sharing that, Jeremy,' I say with a small smile and a nod. He doesn't smile back.

The muscly dreadlocked man speaks next. 'I'm Kyle. In for rape. That's it.' I notice a flash of gold in his mouth and the broad gap between his two front teeth. You could slide a pencil between them.

'Do you want to say any more?'

'Nope,' says Kyle.

Sitting next to him is a man with a shaved, knobbly head, sallow skin and a fierce black beard. I know this is Frank. He has distinctive dark rings under his eyes that look like they have been drawn on with a crayon. A blotchy home-inked tattoo on his forearm spells 'DAD'. He gives an anxious grin and addresses me.

'Hoi, Miss, I'm in for murder. I had sex with a prostitute and killed her and buried her in the garden. And I am sorry.' He drops his bumpy head. 'Oh, and I'm Frank.'

I give him my best therapeutic smile, but his head still hangs.

A man only a few years older than me with a wide, flat face like a dinner plate, light grey eyes and thin, mousy hair speaks next. I know this is Wayne as I have already spotted the self-harm scars tracking his arms like long white slugs. They crawl up both of his pale, hairless arms and under his faded blue T-shirt.

'I'm Wayne. I've bin burgling houses for years and when I was in 'em I raped some women – well, quite a lot of women. And I'm sorry too.'

I attempt a smile, but he will not look at me either.

The fifth prisoner, an enormous tank of a man with a vast belly barely contained by his prison shirt, speaks next. He flattens his goatee beard with huge, tattooed hands. 'LOVE' and 'HATE' are etched across each fat knuckle, and he has a tattooed teardrop dripping from his right eye.

'Andy. I'm in for murder. Of a man.'

'And what have you come to the group to address?' says Daniel.

'My brother's kids … they say I indecently assaulted them. I never – it was just cuddling. And it was ages ago, so I don't really know why I've got to do this group, but I am here or else I am never gonna get out.'

Daniel nods. 'Thanks, Andy, we will get on to why we are here.'

The sixth man in the group has legs so long his grubby prison jeans just reach mid-calf, and a cranium littered with scabs pokes through the top of a circle of greasy brown hair. He also has an overbite. His top row of teeth looks as if it has been bought in a joke shop, like he could pop them out at any moment.

'I killed a child,' he whispers.

The young dreadlocked man, Kyle, gives another disgusted snort.

'We've got a right fuckin' nonce 'ere, lads.'

Andy, the enormous tattooed man, himself convicted of sexual abuse against children, shakes his head and tuts. I can see what is happening and speak up.

'As Daniel says, we have to respect each other; no crime is worse than another,' I tell them.

'Dunno how you can say that, Miss,' says Kyle with a scowl.

I am saying it because that's what we have been taught to say in training. I have thought about it since. Are all crimes the same? Do I really believe that?

'All crimes have victims. Can we really measure the damage and say one is worse than the other?' rescues Daniel.

All three of the facilitators nod, and a couple of the men – Wayne and Frank – do too. Kyle doesn't appear convinced.

We all turn back to the peculiar-looking child killer. His hands are shaking as he expertly rolls his cigarette and lights it, taking a long and audible inhale as if the tobacco contains courage.

'I was a caretaker, at the swimming baths. I took her, did things I shouldn't have, and strangled her. And my name is Nigel.'

'Thank you, Nigel, that is very brave of you to tell us,' I say, remembering the rules about specific praise from my training. We must be careful what we are praising, otherwise it can appear as if we are condoning the offence. Yet we need to praise them to shape behaviour. All humans respond well to praise, sex offender or not. His offence is hideous, and I have no fond feelings for this scruffy murderer, but I do think he is brave to say that in the group with the judgemental Kyle and Andy looking on.

We spend the rest of the session discussing what the course is going to cover, and then we need to set a group contract. Len stands at the flip chart, pen in hand, biting the lid, and Daniel and I facilitate. Confidentiality is the main issue, and they are all fearful about it being broken, especially Nigel. Andy is too. He has boasted on the wing that he has killed a man, pointing to his tattooed teardrop as proof. 'Straight' murder is high on the prison pecking order. However, his past secrets about child abuse will not be as acceptable.

Confidentiality is agreed. They cannot gossip on the wing about each other's crimes. We are unable to have absolute confidentiality as our therapy sessions will be written up into a post-programme report and shared in the risk assessments written by psychologists for the Parole Board. Also, we have an ethical duty that if they disclose information that puts themselves or others at risk then we must report it. Similarly, if anyone gives specific details of an unreported crime, then we must inform the police. They seem to accept it.

When the Cat-A books are signed – the Cat-A book is a small pocketbook owned by each Category-A prisoner, which logs their movements, like a very old-fashioned GPS tracker – and the prisoners have all filed out back to the wing for their lunch and lock-up, we breathe out and put the kettle on for our debrief. I reach for our group log, and we put some thoughts in it about what happened, how the men behaved and any issues we need to keep an eye on.

Clearly Kyle is going to cause us some issues in managing his behaviour. He either sat sullenly or jumped in and interrupted, snorting at an idea if he did not like it. There is already tension between him and Jeremy, the ex-policeman, and Nigel, the man who killed a child. Wayne, the serial rapist, and Frank, the sexual murderer, seemed motivated and are saying they are there because they want to know why they did it. Andy seemed to be saying he was only there because he has to be. I feel drained but ecstatic that it is over, and I have delivered my first session with no embarrassing mistakes.

Daniel hands me a pack of biscuits and tells me with a grin that I have done a great job. I glow warm in his praise. Len is feeling overwhelmed and unskilled, and I can relate to that. I feel we have both relied on Daniel to rescue us at times. The dynamic nature of the group means that we don't know what the prisoners might say next. We must think quickly and give a response that helps them with their learning and moves the group forward. That response must also be open and non-defensive. It is tough work and I feel like I have been juggling rice. I try to tell Len that it is new, and we will learn together, but he does not seem persuaded.

We discuss how the men found it uncomfortable to talk about their offending. I haven't considered this before. TV thrillers usually portray offenders as wily, manipulative and grandiose about their offending. The men in the group were embarrassed and needed to have the information coaxed out of them.

I am worried that the prisoners will find out that this is my first group, although I do not share this thought with Daniel and Len. I am supposed to be the expert. I am supposed to be a psychologist who knows what she is doing with this group of dangerous sexual offenders. I worry they will all look to me for an astute psychological explanation of what they have done and why. And right now I feel like I don't have a clue what I am doing, and that it is only a matter of time before they catch me out.

* * *

Driving home that night in Polly, my trusty little green car, I think about the fact that we have the offences out in the open, and that they are abhorrent. I have sat in a room surrounded by a group of prisoners who have each committed a violent, selfish and repulsive act. I had felt overwhelmed and scared by some of them: the impulsive, psychopathic Kyle, the enormous Andy, the intelligent Jeremy. Wayne and Frank are a serial rapist and sexual murderer, but somehow I felt more at ease with them, perhaps as they seemed so ashamed and anxious in the session. Nigel did not scare me, but his crime is appalling, and I wonder how I am going to cope with hearing all the gruesome details. I will not be going home to watch crime programmes for entertainment. I have heard enough about other people's misery for one day.

CHAPTER FIVE

SEX OFFENDER TREATMENT PROGRAMME IN ACTION

What would cause a married man to sexually assault a child and then kill her? I wonder as I stand by the flip chart holding the pen and fiddling with my key chain. Daniel is sitting down at the other side of the board, leaning forward and listening to Nigel. Each man is considering how their offending fits into the Finkelhor Precondition Model, a theory of sexual offending. This model considers that four preconditions must be in place for a man to commit a sexual offence. It is Nigel's turn, and he is focusing on rolling yet another cigarette, his yellow fingers and overgrown dirty nails working on autopilot. It is the first time I am going to hear about his offence in detail, and we have to try to help him see why he did it. My mouth is parched and my tongue keeps attaching to the roof of my mouth.

I have the first precondition written on the board: '*motivation to sexually offend*'. As we learnt in training, this comprises three factors. First, *Emotional congruence*, which means that an adult feels more comfortable with a child than other adults. This may be due to the need to feel powerful or possibly due to impeded emotional development. Second, *deviant sexual arousal*, which can be as a result of flawed sexual development through exposure to pornography, inappropriate modelling of sexual interests (both particularly relevant in puberty when hormone levels are high) or traumatic child experiences. Third, *blockage*, which, sociologist David Finkelhor argued, can result from a fear of adult relationships/intimacy, relationship problems and poor social skills. The motivation to sexually offend can come from one factor or from a combination of all three.

The whole group looks at Nigel, who lights the roll-up, takes a deep inhale and holds onto the chair arms for support. Nigel explains that he has always felt more comfortable with children. He does not think he is attractive to women. His wife was his first and only girlfriend. He admits that he finds younger teenage girls attractive, and he isn't sure why. He has not been sexually abused.

The group sits and listens as Nigel mumbles his thoughts and I write his answers up on the flip chart. Kyle rolls his eyes at the admission about teenage girls and then sits with his back to Nigel for the discussion, arms crossed, face firmly set on 'bored'. Occasionally one of the group members asks a question and Daniel or I praise them if it makes Nigel think and helps him get the information on the board.

The second precondition is *'overcoming internal inhibitors'*. This is how an individual gets over the socially ingrained message that it is wrong to have sex with children. External factors such as stress, alcohol and exposure to pornography may affect a person's inability to control their deviant sexual desires. Internal factors are the excuses that people tell themselves to make it OK, their cognitive distortions (CDs). CDs enable someone to interpret a situation in a sexual way.

We discover that Nigel told himself that one of the girls from the swimming lessons liked him. She wouldn't have come to see him in the caretaker's office if she did not like him, would she?

Nigel genuinely believes this. Now is not the place to challenge such statements. That will come later in the 'active account' sessions, when we unpick these distortions. I write all his excuses on the board and leave them there, hanging.

'She likes me.'

'She fancies me.'

'Young girls need to be taught about sex.'

'I won't do any harm.'

'She will enjoy it.'

It feels wrong. Of course she did not like him. Why would a young schoolgirl be interested in a strange-looking older man? I can see the other group members thinking the same, pulling faces and shaking their heads.

The next precondition is '*overcoming external inhibitors*'. This is about creating the opening to offend, either through planning or opportunity. It is about finding and isolating a victim. Nigel is unsure how he did this.

'Tell us how you got her alone in the boiler room,' asks Jeremy. He is sharp and good at the questions, and he likes the rest of us to know it.

'I offered her sweets and said she could try one of my ciggies,' replies Nigel with a sniffle. 'But she didn't have to come. She could've said no.'

'Isn't that a CD? *Could* she have said no?' says Jeremy.

He is starting to do our job for us, and that is the aim. They work as a group, and we facilitate it. I write it all up on the board.

'Thanks, Jeremy, great questions. You really helped Nigel there,' I say. He doesn't respond to me.

The final precondition in the model is '*overcoming victim resistance*'. This can take the form of 'grooming' – the gradual creation of trust and dependence, often through the giving of gifts or rewards. It can also be via threats and violence or by incapacitating the victim using drugs or alcohol.

'Well, I definitely wasn't violent,' insists Nigel.

'You bloody killed her, man,' says Kyle, slapping his tobacco tin on the arm of his chair.

'Let's try to remember the contract and the respect we are having for others, Kyle,' I say. He glares at me and turns to Daniel.

'OK. Can you reword that into a question, Kyle?' asks Daniel. He is really calm in these situations, I think.

'Nope,' says Kyle.

'What about the sweets and the ciggies?' asks Frank, looking at Daniel for reassurance.

'Great question, Frank,' Daniel says, and I watch Frank grin to himself.

We talk through how Nigel built up trust with one particular girl over a period of time, offering her the odd sweet or bit of contraband chewing gum and more sweets if she collected them from his office. Eventually he had suggested she bring a friend and they could both try a cigarette. He planned to meet her in the boiler room after their swimming lesson one day, and she came alone as her friend had to go home. As we talk it is almost as if we can see an awareness creeping in for Nigel. He can understand how and why he got there. He did not use physical violence to get her to the boiler room, but he had groomed her over time. The violence came later as an attempt to conceal the crime. He does not go into the details – that is for later in the group – but I feel sad and sick at the same time. I find myself shutting off all thoughts of the victim as a person. I do not like hearing her name as it makes her more real. I cannot allow myself to think about her as someone who had a family, a life, a future ahead of her. I must focus on the man in front of me and do my job.

* * *

It is a much-needed tea break, and I am a bit shell-shocked. I have heard the details of my first child murder. The prisoners seem unaffected and are chatting among themselves, although I notice that Nigel is not included. They have brought in their blue plastic prison-issue cups and the Psychology Department has provided tea, coffee and biscuits. This gives us the unenviable reputation in the prison as being tea-drinking do-gooders.

Jeremy likes to make the tea. He has written out a sheet with everybody's usual order – how many sugars/milk – and had it laminated in the prison library where he works in a trusted role when not in the group. The other prisoners leave him to it. The ten-minute tea break means chatting with the group, and not about treatment. It is hard to find common ground. They are not allowed to ask us personal questions and I have to work hard to keep the boundaries, as they naturally want to know about my life. 'What will your boyfriend say about that?' one of them will ask.

These are subtle yet deliberate attempts to find out more about me. I do not feel that these efforts are sinister, although I must assume the worst. I am finding out their most intimate secrets, and they want to know a bit about mine. Like how I get to work and do I have a boyfriend. We talk about the jail, the weather, current affairs (lifers all get a TV in their cell and they can order newspapers and magazines), what their dream car is (they want to know mine), what meal they miss the most. I get to know almost as much about them as people in these more relaxed ten minutes as I do during the intense therapy sections of the group. I am always on alert, though. I do not like standing with my back to them or reclining too far in my chair in case my suit jacket falls open and they see the shape of my breasts. I do not even like my ankles to be showing and, despite having a fabulous shoe collection at home, would never go into the group with sandals on and my toes on display. My face and hands are the only bit of my bare flesh I allow them to see.

After the break it is Jeremy's turn. Daniel and I swap roles and I become lead facilitator and he the scribe. I feel intimidated by Jeremy as he has picked up on a spelling mistake I have written on the board previously. He is intellectual and likes to boast about the Open University history degree he is completing. He is more than twenty years older than me, so has way more life experience. He says I will understand certain things 'when I am older'. I think he seems disappointed that I am leading and not Daniel.

'So, Jeremy, it's your turn,' I say. 'What do you think is your sexual motivation to offend?'

'Well, I am hoping, given that you are the psychologist, you can tell me,' says Jeremy.

I can feel the familiar flush crawling up my neck and hope he cannot see it. The more I think about it, the further up it creeps. He has put me on the spot, and he knows it. He has not offended against a child, so we dismiss the first factor of emotional congruence.

'What about sexual arousal, an interest in rape?' I ask, knowing that he raped his victim.

Jeremy looks at his neat laces and mumbles to Daniel, 'I was a virgin.'

There is the usual snort and a chuckle from Kyle.

'At least I am not a common criminal. You're just a low-life, scum. I locked people like you up all day long,' Jeremy sneers.

It is uncomfortable, but Daniel is there. 'OK, you two, do we need a time-out? Can we remind you of the contract?'

'Sod the fucking contract. I'm not sitting here with you bunch of twats any longer.' Kyle lurches forward, leaps up and leaves the room, slamming the door behind him.

I jump at the noise. Daniel gets up to follow him. *Please, Daniel. Don't leave me alone in this room.* I feel vulnerable and a tight band of fear grips my chest. Daniel pokes his head out of the door, but he does not leave me. Kyle is standing outside, gesticulating and demanding to go back to his cell.

Five minutes later and another officer has let Kyle back onto the wing. He cannot be persuaded to come back that day and we get on with Jeremy's turn. My heart rate returns to normal, but this has served to remind me that although I might be getting comfortable drinking tea with them and talking about rubbish TV and dream cars, I do not want to be left alone in the room for a second. My mind is on fast-forward, playing 'what if' games. *Imagine if Daniel had left. Would they have trapped me in the room?*

I focus on the session. We establish that Jeremy was a virgin and had wanted to lose his virginity. Prostitutes were suggested by his brother and friends, but he was an 'upstanding' police officer and not about to do this. He has never used rape pornography or been abused or traumatised as a child. He tells us he had a middle-class upbringing with successful parents who treated each other well. He has no interest in rape and thinks it is disgusting.

'I'm telling you. I just wanted normal sex, to lose my virginity. It wasn't rape,' he says.

'That's a CD,' says Frank, eyeing Daniel for confirmation.

Jeremy had taken his shotgun with him when he kidnapped the woman. He had a licence and it was legally owned, he insists on telling us.

'I'm not sure sex can be normal if you've got a gun,' whispers Nigel. I nod at him, thankful for his insightful contribution.

Jeremy is thinking about this. I ask him if he thinks his statement is a CD. He nods at Daniel. This is progress. He acknowledges that there was a strong threat of violence. Overcoming victim resistance, the fourth stage of the model, is also, therefore, very clear.

As the session draws to a close, Jeremy complains about how we are trying to fit him into the boxes of 'Rebecca's clever psychology model'.

'I know what I did; I took a gun, but I don't know why. I am not a deviant. I do not have rape fantasies. I wasn't abused. I just wanted sex and a girlfriend. I was a successful police sergeant. I thought I was going to get some answers on this course.'

I try to explain that hopefully we will get to some answers and that he has done well today, but inside I am thinking: he knows this is my first group and I don't know what I am doing. How am I supposed to know why he committed these dreadful offences? How does a respectable serving police officer end up kidnapping and raping a woman? I do not know. The prisoners file out.

'You OK? You handled him great,' says Daniel, touching my arm and leaving it there for longer than he needs to.

We stay in the group room a long time for our debrief. We get on so well and it feels like there is nowhere else we would rather be than just chatting together, even if it is about sex offenders. I tell Daniel that I am scared he will leave me alone in there with them.

'Never. Not in a million years,' he says. 'I'll always protect you.'

We laugh about how Kyle stormed out and what my face must have looked like. It isn't funny, but it's the only way to deal with it. How we are secretly quite pleased by Jeremy's put-down of him.

I am enjoying spending this time with Daniel. I know he is married. He has mentioned it once in passing, but I can tell he likes me. And I like him. We are spending several intense hours a week together and getting closer each day. We have started going for lunch together, walking into town for a sandwich. Daniel is not my typical type. He is too old, not tall or dark or particularly handsome. And married. Yet there is something that draws me in. He takes every opportunity to flirt with me. He admires my clothes. My figure. He is in awe of my degree. We never flirt in the group and wait until we are alone after the sessions or planning in my office cell. I know that I have to be professional. My job and career are everything. And Len feels like an outsider. It is our group – mine and Daniel's – and I look forward to working with Daniel. He makes me feel safe. We are working with a group of sexual offenders, hearing repulsive, cruel things about sex every day. But there is undoubtedly an attraction building between the pair of us.

CHAPTER SIX

THE HOT SEAT

'I just had a small knife. But I didn't use it. I didn't think that I was really hurting them,' says Wayne.

It is his turn in the 'hot seat', as the men call it. Daniel and I are delivering the session as usual. We are at the 'active accounts' stage of the group where the prisoners must describe in every detail what happened before, during and immediately after their sexual offences. Using the decision-chain method, the group will, hopefully, help each other identify the situations, thoughts, feelings and behaviour that led them to offend. The chain aims to show the clear path the men took, and how the decisions that they made led them closer to the offence(s). The group members' job is to challenge the CDs, enabling the offender in the 'hot seat' to take personal responsibility for what he has done. Our job is to facilitate and record this work, but also to take care of the group processes – the behaviour and interactions of the men, their challenging of each other, the giving of specific praise to encourage appropriate questions and modelling appropriate behaviour (especially important between a male and female facilitator) and social skills. The managing of the group process is as important as the treatment itself: indeed, in many ways, it *is* the treatment.

I feel a heavy anticipation about these sessions. Firstly, there are the gruesome details. We have to read the depositions of the case. These include witness statements from court/police interviews, including the details of the offences in the victims' own words – if they lived. They make for brutal reading. I now decisively avoid any photos, although sometimes they fall out of the files in their entire ghastly colour, like Frank's did.

I read Wayne's huge bundle of depositions (deps) seated at my desk. I take them out of the plain brown envelope. I look at page after page of statements from his victims describing the utter terror and the brutal sexual violence that Wayne inflicted. I read the statements from the doctors who examined the women following the rapes. I read the statements from the police officers arriving on the scene. I want to cry. I know it is him, yet I struggle to match the masked, hooded, armed, dangerous serial rapist, who removed light bulbs, cut phone lines and terrified women at night, with the vulnerable, introverted, dare I say relatable young man I am getting to know. The man who chatters on about sports cars in the tea breaks and loves a custard cream dipped in his tea. How can it be the same person? I read on through the agonising details of the degrading acts, and though I have not eaten I feel a wave of sickness rising into my throat. There is nowhere to go but the old en-suite and I bend over the soiled steel toilet and retch until my throat is sore.

Secondly, I am worried about the blushing problem. It plagues me. In a situation where I have to speak in a large group or have my name called out, the blotchy red blush will appear, racing up my neck towards my ears like spilt red wine on a pristine tablecloth. I have got used to talking in our group by now and have the issue under control in most sessions. However, I am going to be gathering the meticulous details of illegal sexual behaviour, using explicit words, in front of six male, sex-starved, dangerous prisoners and in front of Daniel. As the attraction grows between us, I am more conscious of using sexual words in front of him. How will I say the word 'penis' without going red?

'Small knife … Did not use it. They're CDs, Wayne!' says Frank.

The group is becoming skilled at this now. I write what Wayne said about the knife on the flip chart.

'Looking at it now, Wayne, what do you think?' I say.

'Well, it was only a small knife, and I didn't use it,' he whispers. He cannot meet my eyes.

We spend some time as a group talking about these statements and the impact of any knife, whatever the size, held by a stranger who has invaded your house at night. Wayne is reconsidering his view. That taking the knife *is* using it. That holding onto statements like these makes him feel better about what he has done, but that they are excuses for his actions. His head droops during these conversations; shame seeps out of him like pus oozing from a wound.

We talk through one of Wayne's many offences. He was a long-term house burglar and had broken into a house. By peeping through the curtains, he knew a woman lived there. He watched for a while to make sure there was no man about. When he saw her underwear drying on a rack in the kitchen, he decided that he was going to rape her. He tells us he unplugged the phone in the hall and smashed the light bulb into a towel. At this point I can feel the hairs on my arms and neck develop a life of their own. The woman was sitting on the sofa watching *Coronation Street*. He crept in and hid behind the sofa until the theme tune played as the programme ended.

We explore this time behind the sofa with him and the exact thoughts that were going through his head and driving the behaviour. He can remember talking himself in and out of it, building the courage. Stoking himself like a fire with angry thoughts about all the women who had hurt him. We question, who? He cannot or will not tell us.

Then we take him through the precise details of the sexual offence. Breaking it down into a series of small behaviours helps me distract from the sum of its parts. He does not know the victim's name, and this helps me to detach from her experience and what he is telling us. I do not even think about blushing, despite all the vulgar descriptions of sexual acts. I am too busy doing my job. He speaks at length about what he has done, and I know that it almost matches the victim statements. He is not minimising it; he is telling the truth. It is like he has been waiting to purge his offences and he is vomiting them on the carpet. The contents of his insides are now visible for us all to see and examine.

Wayne said sorry to the victim after the rape and cried. She told him it was OK, and that he should go now.

'Why did she say it was OK?' he asks, shaking his head.

'Why do *you* think, Wayne?' I ask, working on the Socratic questioning.

He thinks about it, cogs whirring.

'Cos I had the knife. Cos she thought I might kill her. She were saving her life, I s'pose, weren't she? Not fort about it like that before, Miss.'

He gets it. Despite everything I have heard, I have to stop myself breaking into the tiniest smile. This is it. We are doing treatment.

* * *

Wayne does not have an easy time during the session. The group is ruthless with him, perhaps because of his honesty and his anxious manner. Any statement he makes that seeks to minimise, justify or excuse his behaviour is jumped on by the group like a pack of hungry wolves and shaken, excuses flying off like bits of discarded flesh, until only the stripped bones of the truth remain. We move on at a sloth's pace. It is edging on the punitive and Daniel and I have to work at protecting Wayne a little from the persistence of the group to get to the facts. They do not hold back, even though they know it will be their turn eventually. In the end we have a completed decision chain of the thoughts, feelings and behaviour that led him to commit a sexual offence. The self-hatred and pity he felt after each rape prevented another attack for a short while, until the pull of the excitement, power, control and sexual release enabled him to go out again and commit another offence. It makes sense, and Wayne is relieved that he can start to understand his past behaviour.

I notice that he is starting to treat me differently, asking my advice and opinions on things and looking at me for reassurance during the session. It is strange to think that he might start to trust me after the way he has treated women. I think we are making real progress. This man is changing his thinking and hopefully, therefore, his behaviour, right before me. It feels like we are taking him apart, examining him and putting him back together again. Will this make him less likely to rape again? I believe and hope it will, or at least that we are starting to help him on that journey. I can feel myself liking him as a person despite what he has done, admiring his traits of openness, honesty, remorse and the desire to understand himself. This is the man whose offences have made me vomit. Yet I am starting to see past his behaviour to the damaged, rather defenceless, child-like man that is hiding beneath.

Louise comes up to the group room to debrief us that day. Most sessions we debrief ourselves. Daniel and I work well together and enjoy spending the extra time in each other's company. Louise is our group supervisor, so she makes the effort to sit in with us once a week and wants to know how it is, hearing all the details.

'Pretty awful,' I say. 'I thought I would be embarrassed saying "penis" in front of the group, but I managed it!'

I am strangely proud. I can see Daniel smiling. This is his second group.

'First time is always the worst. Once it's out there, it's done. You'll be surprised at how they just become normal words after a while.'

I am not sure if that will ever be the case, but I hope so.

'I've got his offence in my head now, though, since I read the deps. It's like a tape running through my skull with it on.'

'Also normal,' says Daniel, and Louise nods. 'Some of them you just can't shake. It's the child offenders that get me. Or when they have no remorse. I don't find Wayne too bad because he's sorry and he did well today. Try to leave that shit here when you go home tonight.'

I appreciate his sentiment but am not sure how I am going to achieve that. I cannot stop thinking about it. It is the thought of someone creeping about the house in the dark with a knife and a gorilla mask. It terrifies me.

That night I sit on the sofa in the tall, old house I share with four other young professional women. The lights are low. The curtains are drawn. It's 7.30 p.m. and the familiar music to the soap opera *Coronation Street* rings out from the TV. I freeze. A droplet of fear trickles down my spine. The hairs all over my scalp stand on end. I can feel hot blood surging and throbbing in my ears, as if they have their own heartbeat. I have an urge to check behind the sofa. What if someone is there, hidden in the dark, masked and clasping a knife, just like Wayne? I sit motionless. Paralysed. I glance at the other girls gossiping and drinking wine. They will think I have gone mad if I start inspecting behind the sofa. But I have to know for my own sanity that no one has crept in while we were cooking dinner. By now I have convinced myself that a rapist is there, and I can hear deep, ragged breathing. My senses are on high alert. I strain to listen over the clattering noise in my chest. I must check. I pretend I am stretching and bring myself to look. Nothing there but a misplaced fluffy pink slipper. No serial rapist waiting to rape us at knifepoint. My senses slacken and I return to the girls in the room. Is this how it's going to be? Will I ever be able to forget what I have heard?

Back in the group room the next day I find it difficult to look at Wayne. Despite the progress he has made and the fact that I have started to see him as a person and not just a serial rapist, the impact on my own life has reminded me of the fear he has caused in others. There must be many women out there who will never again be able to relax on their sofa watching TV, perhaps me included. Yet I must work with him. This is my job. This is what I wanted. I've got my 'true crime' and all its gory details. I tuck all the suffering away in my brain somewhere, like it has iced over, and carry on with the session. I am an old hand at pushing painful things away. Trauma can't hurt if it's in a box with a sealed lid, and I think that this contributes to my hardened shell. My childhood experiences give me the strength and the ability to close down and shut off. They allow me to hear the disgusting details of crimes and not crumble. Although, inevitably, at times I am wobbling.

* * *

In the debrief after finishing Wayne's account, I tell Daniel about my sofa incident. He thins his lips and looks up to the flaking ceiling.

'Can't tell you how angry that makes me, that they are doing this to you,' he says.

He is actually quite handsome in that uniform, I think.

'I just needed to tell someone, and no one else on this earth will understand like you do.'

He looks at me for what feels like a long time. Then right there, in the filthy, sweaty group room, in the aftermath of all the horror we have heard, he kisses me. Softly and slowly.

CHAPTER SEVEN

TROUBLE IN THE GROUP

'Well, you just need to throw the deps at him,' says the Axe Murderer. Bronwyn and I look at each other over our egg sandwiches, eyes wide.

We are having communal lunch in the department and discussing Kyle. We all regularly bring examples and issues to discuss over lunch, especially if we are stuck or it is a tricky case. Kyle is in denial about several aspects of his offence. His victim, who was raped several times by him and his co-defendants, had been clear in her description about what had happened to her. In order to take personal responsibility, and stay in the group, he needs to admit to what he has done. He is resisting and denying one particular type of sexual act: the buggery. Maxine has been doing the SOTP longer than Bronwyn and me. She has a real focus on mining for the truth and getting the prisoners to admit exactly what they have done. Offenders are deselected from treatment if they do not confess to the details of their crimes. Despite my inexperience, I am not comfortable with this harsh approach. I do not feel like we will get the best out of people by treating them this way.

Daniel is there too, having his lunch. I am very aware of his presence. I have not told anybody what happened between us, but I run it through my head on a loop. Now I feel there is no stopping our developing affair. Axe Murderer will disapprove. In my usual way I have partitioned off his marriage behind an internal stud wall in my head. This way I do not have to acknowledge it. I am in too deep. He looks at me across the room, eyes twinkling.

'I think we should just leave it, Rebecca,' he says.

My face displays all sorts of alarm and disappointment.

'Let's not push it with Kyle, I mean. He's never going to admit it and he is so young and so angry. I don't trust him.'

'I'm not sure,' I say. 'I'm going to have another read of the deps before the session. You coming?'

In the relative privacy of my office, standing away from the glass observation panel and pushing me up against the en-suite door, he tells me he cannot leave 'us' if he tries. I should ask about his wife and take the chance to stop it. Stop us both falling into this any deeper. But I am too selfish, and I do not.

Later that night he makes an excuse at the family home and drives over to the shared house. The excited girls have made themselves scarce. There are a hundred frogs hopping in my tummy as I answer the door. I've got freshly shaved legs and my best black underwear on beneath my jeans. It is strange seeing him out of uniform. I let him in with a coy smile, knowing I have passed the point of no return.

In the morning we are back in the group and Daniel and I are running the active account with Kyle. It feels bizarre. There we are, sitting either side of the flip chart, about to listen to a gang rape account. Less than twelve hours earlier we were in my bed. I am paranoid that the group will work it out. Kyle is so blunt that I am fearful he will just shout out, 'Have you two been shagging each other, or what?' Then how will we deal with getting him to admit to anal rape?

I am confused about where the boundaries lie. All I can think about is what happened between Daniel and me. Now I have to think about brutal, abhorrent sex, and we must listen to it together. It is getting very blurred. I am worried about how it will affect me and that I might start thinking about the group and their sexual crimes in bed. I know I have to focus on the job and not let this be a distraction. I'm entitled to a private life, I tell myself, then wonder if this might be CD. I know that it's working so closely on the group that has brought us together, yet I'm determined to keep our relationship out of the group room.

The group is unrelenting in pressing Kyle on the details of his offence for the second session in a row. I tell them what the witness statements say ('throw the deps at him', verbally at least): that the victim reported she had been raped anally and vaginally. Kyle curls his lip and sneers at me.

'I didn't do it. She were fuckin' making it up!' he shouts, slamming his fists on the chair arms again.

'Well, we simply don't believe you,' Jeremy says, arms crossed and thriving in the interrogation-like atmosphere.

'Why would she make it up?' I ask.

Kyle is teetering on the edge of his chair.

'I've fuckin' told you I didn't do it. She is a fuckin' liar, like all women. I fuckin' hate 'em all.'

Kyle shoves his chair back and it clatters on the wall. He stands up, glaring at me, yelling that he has had enough. He lurches towards me. I can smell him. The rage and sweat and cigarette smoke mingling. I shrink back in my chair. He is very close to me, and I can see into his mouth when he shouts. It is a dark red, angry hole, like a bubbling volcano. My palms are sweaty, but I dare not move them on to my rape alarm. Time has slowed down, and I am aware that Daniel is standing up. But Andy, Wayne and Frank are faster. Andy strides over, pushes Kyle aside with his meaty hand and plonks himself between Kyle and me. Wayne and Frank stand either side like sentinels.

'You need to leave,' Andy says. 'You're scaring Rebecca.'

Kyle glares at me and I manage to give a tiny nod. Wayne and Frank move aside to let him pass. He stomps across the room and Daniel follows him out, pressing the alarm bell on the way as Kyle starts punching the wall outside the door. The bell goes off like a fire alarm on steroids.

I can see Daniel outside the door, but now I am alone with the rest of them. One of them could shut the door and five sexual offenders will have me hostage. *Will they really take this chance?* I have been warned time and time again never to let myself be in this situation. *Why has Daniel left me?* Andy plods to his chair and Wayne and Frank find theirs. Frank asks me if I am OK.

Outside I can hear the thundering, urgent feet of officers on the run as they swarm like bees to help Daniel with Kyle. They bundle Kyle off, arm up his back as he continues to rant and swear at them. I look at the men sitting there, unperturbed, rolling cigarettes and waiting for the group to start again. No one has any intention of taking me hostage. They are used to the outbursts and violence. They live with it every day. But this is the first time that I have felt in real, immediate physical danger from a prisoner. And they literally shielded me. I hadn't expected it, especially from Andy, who is a giant of a man. When he stands up the room darkens. He fills the door and has to drop his huge, wide head as he comes in.

There is no doubt he would have dealt with Kyle. The dynamics are changing. Wayne and Frank moving from perpetrators of violence against women to my protectors. And emotionless Andy, who insists that he shouldn't be here, that it is a waste of time, has now shown a more loyal, caring side. The bond in the group continues to build. My trust in them has grown a little more, although I still feel unable to turn my back to write on the flip chart. Just in case.

That night, as we are lying in my single bed, Daniel and I talk about our day. He has made another excuse at the marital home. He is annoyed with me for pushing it too far with Kyle, saying that he had no choice but to leave me in the room with the men. Talking about the men in bed is a crossing of all sorts of lines and it feels wrong. And so we agree: absolutely no talking about the group in bed; keep the relationship out of the group room and out of the prison. I am still worried about the details of the crimes creeping into our sex life, and I wonder if Daniel is too. Neither of us says anything.

We carry on with our affair, sneaking illicit nights at my house and going out for lunch. Our secret is so heavy and intense, and in the end I must tell someone, and of course it is Bronwyn. She has seen the flirting and intimacy growing between us and has already guessed. I never question whether I am doing the right thing or think about the consequences for anyone else. I am drawn in. Overwhelmed and besotted. He isn't a drop-out and he does not feel like a fixer-upper. I am in a relationship with a real man for the first time. With Daniel, I feel loved, idolised and important. First choice, perhaps for the first time in my life.

And we are not the only ones mixing work and pleasure, finding love in the prison. The new Labour government is making more money available across the prison service for offending behaviour programmes. There is an influx of fresh young female psychologists straight out of university entering the prison to deliver programmes. Prison officers are being recruited off the wings to join the Psychology Department and help to meet the rapidly growing delivery targets. It is a breeding ground in the making and many of the new psychologists eventually end up in relationships with married officers. Like many office environments, workplace affairs become the norm in the prison, and we all carry on with our jobs regardless.

These relationships are no doubt based on sex between impressionable young women drawn to the excitement and middle-aged men searching for a thrill and an escape. On another level, there is more to it. We are all in a unique situation, in that we understand the extraordinary environment we work in like no one else can. Working in a maximum-security prison is like being in a private members' club. There are strict rules about who can be in it and a loyal bond forms between the members, despite the chauvinism. We spend more time with the officers than their spouses do, and to them we are young, fresh, intelligent and available. The opposite of their middle-aged and marriage-weary wives. To us they are impressively mature, real men in uniform whose ultimate role at work is to protect us from other bad men. We are irrepressibly drawn to each other, and like the meteorite that finished the dinosaurs, there is simply no stopping it.

To everyone's surprise, after a short spell in the Segregation Block for punching the wall, Kyle returns to the group. He strides into the room, plops down in his usual chair next to me and says, 'I did it.'

I look at Daniel, eyebrow raised in a slight 'I told you so' expression, and do my very best to smile at Kyle and thank him for his honesty.

I feel wary of Kyle that day, but after a discussion, the group agrees he can stay. We spend some of the rest of the session talking through Kyle's admission. It feels like a victory, although I am not sure what of. We are pleased he has admitted to the anal rape, but this alone is not going to stop him from raping again. I have seen that he is still angry, impulsive and aggrieved with women, and still capable of losing his temper. His actions that day were like watching a repeat of his offending. I know this is what is known as offence-paralleling behaviour and is an indication that risk is still present.

CHAPTER EIGHT

MAKING PROGRESS

After the tea break it is Frank's turn. He is very pale, like he needs a pint of blood. He tells us that he thought about what his CDs might be before he came to the session, and as he can hardly read and write he has them all in his head. I still want to know if he raped his victim before he killed her.

He gives his account. His girlfriend had gone away, he had been out drinking with his dad and left to pick up a prostitute. He did not have the money to pay her up front and so she refused to have sex with him. The group is pushing him about his thoughts. Frank takes a deep breath and tells us that he is going to be honest. He was 'going to have a shag, no matter what she said'. He explains how he had been embarrassed to admit to the rape before. Frank did not want his girlfriend at the time, or his dad, to know what he had done, and it had just got harder to say 'I did it' as time went on.

Frank says he did not mean to kill her, but when the victim tried to leave the car, he lost all control. He describes the 'red mist' that fell over him.

'It's like it wasn't me. Like I was watching moiself strangle her.'

He speaks about trying to conceal the evidence and the burial of the victim's body. He drove home, borrowed a shovel from a neighbour and dug a hole in the back garden in the middle of the night. Did he not think he might get caught? He wasn't thinking, he says. He was in a blind, useless panic. He even returned the shovel the same night, hands and clothes covered in mud. He describes his angst and rushing around trying to clean up, scrubbing the car and the footwell, spilling water and bleach everywhere. Desperately trying to destroy the DNA evidence. Frank says he knew that he would get caught but did not know what else to do. He took the light bulbs out of the lamps and hung the quilts up in the windows so it would appear as if there was no one in. He paced the house, fear rising, and chain smoked. Eventually there was a knock at the door. The neighbour had called the police. He describes being so relieved it was over that he admitted murder to the officers, right there on the doorstep.

'Well, that rarely happens!' says a knowing Jeremy.

Frank's story strikes me. He has described the impending, heavy dread with such clarity that I feel like I have been there with him. Given that I have seen the photographs too, I can picture it all in my head, like it's my story too. And I understand at that point why he behaved as he did with the shovel and all that followed: he literally wasn't thinking straight. He could not. He had lost the power to do so. Overtaken by self-preservation, intense emotion, arousal and sheer panic, his thinking brain went offline. Who can say how anyone would behave in that situation?

A couple of nights later I dream that I have killed the postman and buried him in the front garden. In my dream I know this is a hopeless place to bury anyone and realise I will be found out. I am hanging sheets at the windows, taking bulbs out of the lights, and I feel the dense dread, the inescapable, dragging feeling that I am going to be caught and put in prison for life. I am waiting for the police to knock at the door. I wake up and the heavy, frightened sensation is still there. Have I really killed someone? It takes a few seconds for it to dissipate even though I know it is a dream. I am reliving Frank's offence.

The group crawls through the active accounts. Jeremy is difficult, pointed and resistant to questioning from anyone that he sees as not worthy of asking him questions, which is pretty much all the group, especially Kyle and Wayne, who have long criminal records. He likes to try to engage in a psychological debate with me as a distraction method from talking about his offending. Yet he does genuinely want to understand what happened and why. With some persistent questioning, he is beginning to see that the offence was always going to be rape and that the idea that it was going to be consensual sex is a false notion that he holds onto. That taking a gun and kidnapping the victim is violence; therefore, even if he managed to 'talk her round to being his girlfriend', it would still be rape. He is intelligent enough to see this, but still struggles to understand how he got to this point. He cannot see himself as a rapist. He says that the murder of the dog walker who disturbed him was down to shock, instinctive reaction and police training. Jeremy struggles to give up the role of being a policeman. It is such a crucial part of his personality. He cannot identify with being a criminal and complains about 'sitting in a room full of burglars', even though he has two life sentences. We still have a way to go with him.

Andy remains defensive and reluctant to engage in talking about his sexual offending behaviour. He sexually abused his brother's two daughters several years ago and the offending was only revealed when they were adults. He constantly says it was 'nothing', 'it only happened once', 'they did not come to any harm as they both got married and had children'.

'CD, CD, CD!' the others will call more and more loudly, like frenzied parrots, getting more irritated each time. He just shrugs his shoulders as we write up his statements on the board. The group get fed up with him, but he is good at asking questions of the others, sitting there in silence for much of the session and then coming out with a gem that makes everyone think. He would far prefer to talk about the murder he is serving the life sentence for. We do not get much closer to understanding his behaviour, aside from discovering that he has never had a close relationship. His vast size puts everyone off. 'Do you think that frightens people away?' volunteers one of the group members. He shrugs his mammoth shoulders, but I think I see a glimmer of interest.

After a night out with my housemates one evening we come stumbling home in the dark to find our front door swinging open. The tell-tale smashed glass panel tells us all we need to know. We have been burgled. We stand on the stone step, all five of us in flimsy, shiny dresses, suddenly strangely sober and not sure of what to do.

'We need to call 999,' I say. 'Surely, we'll be a priority?'

The door swings further inwards with the wind and we can see into the shadowy hallway. The scattered glass triangles on the patterned tiles give off a yellow glint from the streetlamp. There are no lights on in the house and the stairs loom up and away out of the narrow hallway and into total darkness.

'Perhaps we should go in,' says one of the girls bravely. 'I'm freezing my bits off standing here.'

A collection of offences swoops into my brain. Firstly, Wayne, who burgled, lay in wait like a fox and raped. Has someone smashed the lights and holed themselves up inside, waiting for us? I have worked with other men doing SOTP assessments and parole reports. What about the man who broke into student houses and waited under the bed for the young woman to return? He raped her several times after taping her mouth so she would not scream and alert her friend in the room next door. I remember the man who had been disturbed in a burglary by a mother and her daughter. He bound them both together with their own dressing gown cords and murdered them with a hammer. I have countless examples in my head of men committing appalling crimes in the homes of women. My brain is a jumbled mess of violent and sexual offences. There might be someone in there now, waiting under the bed, or behind the sofa, with tape or a knife or a hammer and wearing a gorilla mask.

'We can't go in,' I say, my heart thumping as my fight-or-flight reaction kicks in, pushing blood around my body. I do not even feel cold now. 'Far too dangerous. There could be a serial killer or a rapist in there. Or both.'

'Not everyone is a serial killer, Rebecca,' says another girl. 'That's just your bloody awful job. It'll just be kids trying to nick our TV. Loads of houses get broken into round here. Happens all the time.'

Not in my cases, I thought. I have never dealt with a petty burglar before, if there is such a thing. There is always a sexual motive and/or a dreadful, violent ending for my victims.

Suddenly there is a loud, sharp thump from deep inside the house, like someone has fallen off a bed. The beam of a torch appears, snaking down the stairs. Desperate feet clatter down behind the glare of the torch and two lanky, hooded men rush past us, rucksacks on their backs, heads down. We have disturbed them on the job. I scream. They jump the low wall and are gone, sprinting up the street. I can hear one laughing and whooping as they escape into one of the rabbit-warren alleys that link the rows of back-to-back terraces and cobbled streets in this treeless suburb of the city.

We are all rattled. None of us expected to see the burglars. We hang onto each other and call 999 from the garden. We do not know if there is anyone else in the house, we say. Please can they come. Right away. Please. We have seen the burglars. We are scared and shaking and smoking, and I cannot help but think of Wayne again. Did they have knives? Is there someone else lying in wait inside? Is it a trap?

It is the early hours on a Saturday night, we live in a city and we have reported that the burglars have run away. The police will be a while. We huddle together on the stone garden wall under the streetlamp for an hour or so. It gets colder. We run out of cigarettes. No one else appears, either from inside or in a police car. One of the girls says she is going in before we all die of hypothermia. Armed with an old washing-line pole from the garden, we creep in, stilettos crunching on the glass, and put the lights on. As a fivesome we tiptoe into every room, clinging together for safety. I make the girls check under every bed, behind every sofa and in every cupboard and wardrobe. I even look in my laundry basket.

There is no one there, but our belongings have been rifled through. Drawers have been emptied and several small valuable-ish items are missing. We make cups of strong tea, eat toast and Marmite and wait for the police. I cannot go to bed. I tell myself they are only kids and nothing like the men I am dealing with every day. It isn't a knife-wielding rapist that has targeted us. Yet I am so perturbed that someone has been in the house, in my bedroom, and has seen my underwear. More offences stream into my head at the sight of my ransacked, scattered clothes. I poke at my knickers and bras with a coat hanger to make sure that they are not covered with semen or urine or faeces like I have read about in the prison files. Now I am a real victim, although no one has actually touched me. How much worse it must be for the victims of the men I am working with. Those women must have been utterly terrified. It gives me goosebumps just thinking about it and I'm shivering uncontrollably, despite us putting the gas fire on full. Eventually the police arrive, take a statement and depart. We all peel off to bed. I change the bedding and lie there sleeplessly. I listen to every tiny noise the old creaky house lets out, straining to hear and identify them. I imagine each to be a tread on the stairs or the sound of the patched-up front door being opened. Sleep is elusive that night and for many nights more.

Back in the familiar group room with Len on Monday morning, without giving too much away about my personal circumstances, I tell the group about the burglary.

'Can't believe someone's done that to you, Miss. Find out who it is – I'll have 'em sorted,' Wayne says.

I look in utter disbelief at the man who has burgled and raped many women in their own homes. I catch myself and try to control my features. How can he be so two-faced, after what he has done?

I am interested in their responses. They now have a real-life victim in the room. Jeremy gives me some statistics about how likely the police are to catch the burglars – very unlikely – and Kyle yawns and asks when we are going to get on with the session. Some of them are rattled about what has happened to me – Frank and Wayne and Andy. Even Nigel looks concerned in his own quiet, unobtrusive way. Maybe because of the programme and the fact that they are starting to think about their actions and their impact on others, they do not like hearing about what has happened to me. It is like a personal injury and an insult to them. Frank and Wayne have deep issues with women and yet they are starting to see me in a different way and are looking out for me. And I am re-evaluating them too. Some of these sexual offenders have the capacity to care.

The last person to undertake his active account is Nigel. He has self-selected to take the last turn in the 'hot seat', probably as he sees his own offence as the worst crime in our group. While we have tried to teach and model to the offenders that all crimes have victims and there is no hierarchy, this is not how it feels underneath. I just do not say it out loud. The other members indicate that they feel this too through the odd sly comment and the fact that Nigel never gets his tea first at the break. He accepts this: his self-esteem and position in the group is too low to challenge it. Child killers have a harsh time in prison, and although the group has developed a level of camaraderie, I don't think anyone is looking forward to Nigel's account.

'I've been thinking about where it all came from,' he mumbles, head bowed, voice soft.

There is some shuffling of feet.

'Always had an interest, you know, in girls. I was born like it.'

'We all have that interest, man,' says Kyle with a wink. 'Fucked a fair few birds in my time. Oh … can't say that now, can I? I've got to show ree-spect' – he puts both hands in the air and draws speech marks with his fingers – 'for women. Although fuck knows why – they ain't never shown no respect to me. Only good for one thing. Hey, lads?'

Not for the first time in the group, I am reminded of some of the wing officers. I have overheard the lurid tales of sexual conquest on a Monday morning. The stories of 'top' nights out that result in the 'pulling and shagging of birds'. Friday nights in the local town for the officers consist of a beer-sodden crawl down the slope of the main street where bars selling pints for a pound intermingle with the pound stores. A pound will get you a lot in this gritty Northern town and it's a good job, as unemployment is high. Popular activities at one sticky-floored establishment include ingesting shots of tequila in the 'dentist's chair', the sole aim to render the drinker incapable of basic bodily functions, such as walking. Nearby, the pub with topless barmaids is particularly well frequented. The officers hunt in packs like greedy hyenas. Their prey are young women in short skirts, their white stilettos clashing with purple mottled legs. The women also move in packs, perhaps for protection, but there is no escape from the pull of the officers with their macho stories of bravery and full-time jobs. I have no idea how I am going to try to teach Kyle to think and act differently when this is what he hears when he returns to the wing. The problem feels insurmountable. I must try to help the prisoners in front of me, but the backdrop for our rehabilitation efforts is incongruous at best, and collusive and perpetuating at worst.

'Enough, Kyle. Think about the contract. Think about Rebecca 'ere. You can't say that,' says Len with a stern glare.

Kyle mutters something under his breath.

'I didn't catch that. Shall we carry on wi' session?' says Len. 'Apologise, lad. And mind yer manners.'

'Sorry, Miss,' says Kyle sarcastically. 'It's like being a child in 'ere, ain't it, fellas?' trying to drum up support from the others.

The men ignore him.

'Let's carry on,' I say, wary of Kyle. I know that we should be challenging these attitudes that are so clearly related to his offending, but I also do not want to lose what Nigel has just said. Group work always feels like spinning china plates, and I need more hands.

'Yeah,' says Nigel. 'So, I always liked girls, it's just that when I grew up my interests did not. They stuck in time, like.'

Nigel explains that he sees his paedophilia as a curse and has known about it since he was a young teenager. His marriage was a sham, and he was trying to conceal his true sexual interests, which is in young girls. He is worried that he can never change, as he has no interest in adult women or men. Nigel sees himself as disgusting and is ashamed of his behaviour. Surprisingly, he talks openly about it and, despite not liking what they hear, the group respect his honesty and listen. I do notice that Kyle cleans his fingernails with a pen lid the entire time.

Nigel's offending pathway becomes clearer. It was all planned. The job at the swimming baths was to get him nearer to children. He found adult women threatening. He felt more at ease 'having a relationship' with a child and told himself this was what he was building with the victim – although he now understands it to be grooming. We take him through the exact details of what happened that day and what he said. Finally, we move on to the sexual assault. I ask for Nigel's thoughts and feelings and behaviour throughout every aspect of the sexual offence and Len charts them up on the board.

It is an unusually hot summer day and airless in the group room. I can see patches of sweat leaking from Nigel's armpits onto his grubby shirt and he keeps wiping his head with his sleeve. Len opens the windows as far as they will go, about six inches, and we return to the boiler room and the victim. Nigel describes panicking after the sexual assault when the victim says she will 'tell', and he cannot bear for his wife to find out or to lose his job. We take him through the murder. He strangled the victim with her pants. His story echoes with Frank's as he describes the panic, the hiding of the body, returning home to his wife and trying to eat his tea. Waiting for the inescapable *bang-bang* of a police officer's fist at the door.

Frank nods as Nigel describes it all and asks him some searching questions about his behaviour and what he was thinking. He is relating it to his own experience. Nigel is also learning from Frank, and these two are the experts in the room on sexual murder, not us, the facilitators. There is some of the usual victim-blaming and CDs around the offence – 'she knew what she was doing', 'I just wanted to teach her about sex', 'it isn't going to hurt'. It does not take much of the Socratic questioning to unpick these and for Nigel to see his offence for what it is. The session is tough for everyone, but again I note the relief in Nigel as it progresses. It is as if he is becoming lighter as he shares his load and he looks like he might levitate off the chair. Again, with my focus on the task, my brain whirring away like the code-breaking Enigma machine, thinking of the next question, how I should respond, managing the group, I can disconnect from the raw and sickening details of the crime. A bit like rubbing your head and patting your tummy, it's tricky to do the two tasks at once.

During the tea break, when Nigel is grateful to receive his sugary tea first and sits picking a scab on his head, and as we are chatting about something light and irrelevant to try to alleviate the tension, there is a loud buzz and a small shriek. Andy, all twenty-plus tattooed stone of him, is clambering up on his chair. Wayne, next to him, drops down and claws the air. Frank leaps from his chair, ducking and running away from the windows. There is a wasp.

I take a moment and stand up with my manual.

'Don't worry, guys,' I say and, after a few swoops, splat the now irate, similarly imprisoned wasp in the middle of the flip chart. 'Panic over.'

I have rescued two frightened murderers and a serial rapist from a single wasp. It has relieved the pressure in the room.

'I've not got long for debrief,' sighs Len when we are done and a smelly, damp but relieved Nigel has traipsed out with the rest of them for lunch. The boiled veg and cheap meat wafts up from the kitchens and reminds me of school dinners.

'I'm detailed back on't wings for bang-up before I get me snap, and I'm starving already.'

'That's a shame – about the bang-up, I mean, not your lunch … They need to sort your shifts out – you can't just go back up there now after that. You need to come down from the session a bit. That was tough, what Nigel said,' I say.

'Aye, but I've got no choice. Worst bit'll be they see me coming off here and ask me how the beast counselling has gone.'

'Who? The prisoners?'

Len shakes his head.

'No, the staff. It's drilled into us to hate the nonces. They don't get why I want to do this. Mind you, when I 'ear what we've 'eard today, not sure I do either.'

I look at Len, who is now biting his nails for comfort as usual. Big, tough, steady-as-a-rock Len who served in the British Army for twenty-plus years, protected the Queen and likes nothing more than a pint or three and banter with his mates. Nobody should have to hear what we have heard today in such appalling detail.

'I've seen some stuff in me time, but nowt like this,' and he shakes his shaved head in utter despair.

I desperately want to make him feel better, but there is no brushing away what we have just heard and examined in every microscopic and unspeakable detail. Why *are* we going into it in such detail? I wonder.

'It's tough, really tough, but we've got to remember why we are here. We're trying to stop them from doing it again. Save the next child. We can't do anything for Kelly, but we can stop Nigel from doing it again. If he ever gets out.'

'I know, that's what I do try 'n' think about, just sometimes you can't believe what people do to each other. Anyhow, I've gotta go – got bang-up.'

And off he lumbers to fulfil his prison-officer duties, head clearly spinning. I go to find Bronwyn for lunch. She always knows exactly what to say to make me feel better after a tough session.

CHAPTER NINE

THE PROFESSOR AND VICTIM LETTERS

A tiny, snowy-haired man with milky blue eyes and skin like a frayed old treasure map is sitting in our group. In his tracksuit and child-sized white trainers he blends in expertly among the men. He is an eminent, world-renowned professor of sexual-offender research and treatment, and he wants to observe a session of the English SOTP. I had expected the distinguished professor to bustle in dressed in a smart suit and to be somewhat condescending. Instead, he trotted in, all smiles in his trackpants, extended a freckled arm and said, 'Hi there, I'm Rob,' as if I might be mistaken as to who he was. I have been reading his papers and books throughout my university studies and my entire career. I was not anticipating that he would be so humble. He is the grandfather of our field and there is nothing he does not know about the research or treatment of sexual offenders.

The prisoners are on their very best behaviour, sitting still and waiting for the group to start. There is no swearing, no interrupting each other or messing about. The usual banter has been dialled down in an unspoken pact. It is as if they want to show the professor that we have been good parents and taught them how to behave. Daniel and I are nervous. The men do feel a little like our children and I want to show off the group and how well it is working. But my old demons are there too. It will be obvious it is my first group. The professor has been running treatment for years and is the expert. He is certain to find out that I have no idea what I am doing and am winging the whole thing. I wish that he were sitting in on another group – Alex's perhaps. She has far more experience than me and is a proper psychologist.

'As you know, everybody, Professor Bunting is with us today, observing how we run the group here in England,' I say, voice trembling a little, blush under control with the trusty polo neck.

Frank and Wayne grin at me in support, willing me to do well. They can tell we are under pressure and do not want to let us down.

'Today you are going to read out your victim letters. Who would like to start?' I ask.

We have finished the active accounts and are in the second block of the course – the victim empathy sessions. Last session, after we watched videos of real-life victims talking about the impact of sexual violence on their lives, we asked the men to write a letter to their own victims for in-cell work. These letters will never be sent, but are a task designed to encourage the men to think about the harm they have caused their own victims and their families.

Surprisingly, Nigel, who always holds back as if his rightful place in the group and in life is last, volunteers to go first. He pulls out his letter with quivering hands.

'I've written to Kelly's mam,' he says, turning to me for reassurance.

There is self-imposed silence in the room as he reads it through in a whisper. In the short letter Nigel says he is sorry, so sorry. He has done a very terrible thing and he feels very awful about it. He thinks about it every day and wishes it had never happened. At the end he signs it off, 'Best wishes, Nige,' and asks that 'one day I hope you will forgive me'. He sits there, head down, waiting for our reaction.

Daniel looks at me. I know he is checking who is going to lead. I move my head a fraction, and he understands.

'Any thoughts on that?' he asks the men, in tune with me as ever; there's no need for words.

Eager to please, the group launch into a self-managed, turn-taking discussion about how it is a good letter, but that Nigel comes across as too sorry for himself. Even Kyle is behaving for now.

'And don't ask for forgiveness, man,' says Kyle. 'No one in their right mind ain't ever gonna forgive you after what you did. Especially not her mam.'

Nigel is downcast, but as usual takes any criticism without retort. We discuss forgiveness and the group agree that they do not deserve to be forgiven and it would be wrong to ask for it.

'We shunt be asking for nuffing, should we, Miss?' says Wayne to me, but looking at Professor Bunting, who gives him a wrinkly smile in acknowledgement. Wayne puffs up his chest like a showy bird trying to attract a mate.

Jeremy goes next and, checking to make sure he has the professor's full attention, reads out his extensive and articulate letter in his finest Queen's English. He has written to the victim of the rape about why and how the offence happened and that he understands that life will be very difficult for her. He finishes by saying:

> I think I have a good cognitive understanding of who may have been affected, and the ripple effect. I see my offending like a stone going into a pond and sending out waves and this will have been wide-ranging. All the victim's family and friends, and the dog walker's family, friends, neighbours, work colleagues, the ambulance crews and the police officers first on scene will have all felt terrible, just terrible.

'Had to get the cops in there though, didn't you, man?' says Kyle with a wink.

He seems the least affected by our illustrious guest.

'Well, I am proud to say I am a long-serving police sergeant. So I do rather know the procedures,' Jeremy says, eyeing the professor.

'Is this the first time you have thought about the effect on the police and emergency services, Jeremy?' I say, kicking myself for the closed question as soon as it is out of my mouth, and he answers 'yes'.

'Can you tell us a little more about the emotions that the victims might have been feeling, apart from terrible?'

This is a better question to show the professor I have some competence, although technically, if Jeremy is in challenging mode, he can again just answer 'yes'. Jeremy lets me off the hook but is struggling with the nuances of the task. His face is devoid of emotion, and he cannot say anything more about how the victims might have felt. It is like he has been plopped onto the planet from outer space and given only half of the human functioning instruction manual.

Wayne's letter surprises me. This is the man who, back in his active account, could not see how the presence of a knife, even though he did not 'use' it, will have affected his victims. Now it is as if a plug has been uncorked and his feelings come tumbling out like Smarties from a tube. His letter goes something like this.

To ALL my victims and there familys and all the 10000s peeple to do with my awfle and teerble crims.

This is Wayne here. i am SO SO SO sorry for what i do to you all braking into your houses and braking your trust and braking and taking your things and hurtin you ALL very badly. i am in prison now whare I deserv to be and i shud be here until i am dead and it will not be long enuff to say sorry and to Punissh me for what i have done to you All and i am on the SOTP now wich is a good Program for bad peeple like me and I am lerning about why i do it all and lerning evry thin about what is rong with me so i do not and will NEVER EVR do any fin like this again and not hert any more peeple ever evr again as long as i live. i hve Rabeca and dan and Len helpin me to stop all the Badnss in me and i can feel it Stoppn now as I am lerning all the fings about why it happned. i no i took a nife and i no that that is very scary for you All and even tho i no i wasnt gonna use it you All do not no that and so i am very very sorry for that to and you all must have been very fritend and i no that now cos of the SOTP and i wish I had nevr done it all or takn that nife or worn that orful mask. I wsh i can tern back time and make it all go awey. I will nevr rite to u All again.

WAYNE

Wayne looks at his knees for a long time after reading out his letter and a solitary, snotty tear drops onto his dirty jeans.

'Why are you crying, Wayne?' I ask.

I thought it important to know: is this for him, or for his victims? It is odd watching a prisoner cry.

'I'm just so ashamed and I never knew 'bout all the damage I have done to all those people and how I can't never take it back. And I wish I could. So badly,' he sniffles. 'And I haven't cried since I was at school, and I am not crying now. This course is so fuckin' hard. Really sorry, Miss, for the language,' he says.

It is like Wayne is turning himself inside out, and watching him feels as intrusive as open-heart surgery.

'I know it's tough, Wayne, it's supposed to be, but you are doing really well,' says Daniel. 'What do the rest of you think about Wayne's letter?'

'It is really good, mate,' says Frank.

'Yes,' says Nigel. 'Much better than mine.'

'Well done, Wayne,' says Jeremy. 'Did you think about the effects on the emergency services, like I did?'

Frank has written a brief letter to the victim's parents. He apologises over and over, says he feels so guilty and that he is doing treatment to understand himself better and make sure it never happens again. The group praise his letter.

Professor Bunting speaks for the first time. 'Guilt is a wasted emotion, folks.'

Eight faces turn to him as we all digest this unusual nugget.

'Why is that? Professor, Sir,' asks Jeremy, almost bowing in his chair.

'Your energy is better spent on something else. The guilt is for you and not your victims.'

I think about that and what an interesting perspective he has raised. I have imagined that this victim empathy work is to try to make them feel guilty for what they have done for the sake of their victims. They are all murderers, child molesters and rapists. Shouldn't they be feeling *guilt-ridden*? Yet Professor Bunting may have a point. It feels like an indulgence for them all to feel guilty. Responsible, certainly. Sorry, yes, undeniably. Determined not to do it again, absolutely. But perhaps guilt is, as he says, a self-serving waste of emotion and energy if you think about it. I'm not entirely convinced, but the group lap it up.

'Thank you, Your Honour,' says Jeremy. 'It all makes so much sense now *you* have explained it to us.'

I trip straight into my usual thoughts … *It is obvious that what this group needs is an experienced psychologist. One that can provide shrewd psychological, crystal-ball-type insights all day long. We have spent all session on this topic, and the professor has only contributed one astute sentence and has made them all think on another level. I am definitely going to be found out here*, went my string of familiar automatic thoughts forever on speed dial.

We move on and Kyle relaxes back into his chair and reads his short letter out next.

> Hello Miss (soz I can't remember your name!),
> I am sorry I hurt you, I feel really bad about it. I am doing the SOTP for my sins. I hope my Co-ds [co-defendants] are too, coz they really needs it!
> From Kyle

'That's proper crap, man. And you're blaming your co-ds,' says Wayne. 'And *do* you feel bad? Didn't think you gave a shit.'

'Appalling,' scoffs Jeremy. 'You have absolutely no victim empathy at all Kyle.'

Kyle shrugs his shoulders. 'Well, what more d'you want me to say? I've said I'm sorry. I've got life. Mr Professor here just said I shunt feel guilty.'

It is Andy's turn next. His letter is also brief.

> Dear Victims,
> I am sorry for what I am supposed to have done all those years ago, really sorry. BUT I know you have both got on with your lives and had children, so hopefully it isn't that bad. I will be in here for a very long time

because of what I did. Say Hi from me to your dad if
you see him!

Love from Uncle Andy

The group looks at Andy like he has just grown another
body part.

'That is proper shit,' Wayne says, shaking his head.

'It really is,' says Nigel, daring to comment for the
first time. He rarely criticises the others; it's almost as if
he feels he does not have the right.

'OK, group, thanks for your feedback. What exactly is
it about the letter that you want to comment on?' says
Daniel.

'Blames the victims. *Calls* them victims, loike. Says it
isn't that bad. Feeling sorry for himself about being in
prison. And no feelings for them,' rattles off Frank,
counting the points on his fingers.

I beam with pride.

'As if they will say hoi to their dad from you – they
probably wish you were dead.'

'And everything before the "but" is bullshit,' says the
professor. 'You've got to watch out for that one in life.
Catches everyone out.'

Now we all look at *him* like he has grown an extra
limb. I have never heard anyone be so directive in treatment before. We try to ensure every question is Socratic,
and sometimes it feels like we are not getting to what
needs to be said. I think I might try being a bit more

directive myself, although maybe they won't take it from me. Certainly, Jeremy will not.

After the group has filed out – Jeremy insisting on shaking the professor's hand – Daniel and I await his feedback.

'Y'all did a great job,' he says, rocking up out of his chair and observing us with his cloudy eyes. 'You two clearly have a relationship. Those guys are doing real good. Apart from the young guy and the big guy, of course. They've got a way to go.'

I mull over his words. What does he mean, 'a relationship'? Has he worked us out? Our affair is still clandestine and a secret from the group, Axe Murderer and everyone but Bronwyn. Is he so wise and perceptive that he has us figured out in one session? Probably. He is a world-famous psychologist after all, and he shoots from the hip.

'He just means our rapport. We work together really well in the group, you know, as facilitators,' says Daniel when I ask him about it later. 'Don't worry, Rebecca. We're doing a great job, he said so.'

I am not sure I believe this, but the little professor is heading for his plane, so our secret is safe for now.

CHAPTER TEN

RE-ENACTING THE OFFENCES

I am kneeling beside Nigel on the scratchy, stained, familiar carpet of the group room. I have never been as near to a prisoner before. I can smell the years of malodorous Victorian prison emanating from him, like haze off a stagnant pond. His eyes are squeezed shut and he is trembling. Close up, his skin is a waxy, creamy yellow and it reminds me of the dead bodies I have seen while working in nursing homes in my teens. I can see the individual crusty scabs on his scalp, and the blackheads on his spongy nose.

'What is happening now, Kelly?' I whisper.

'He's touching me … down there,' mumbles Nigel.

'Do you want him to?'

'No!'

I thrust the marker pen into the top of his thigh and he jumps like he has been stung. His leg is shaking. I push it in again. Not too hard, but hard enough.

'This goes on for one minute, Kelly.' I look at my watch and time it. 'How does it feel?'

'It's hurting, it's horrible, what is he doing?'

'What can you smell, Kelly?'

'Him. And he stinks of cigs. He's disgusting.'

'What can you see?'

'Nothing, I've got my eyes shut. Can't open them.'

'What can you hear, Kelly?'

'His disgusting breathing.'

'What are you thinking?'

'I want him to stop. I want my mam.'

'What is happening next, Kelly?'

'He's gonna kill me.'

I lie a rolled-up prison jumper across Nigel's neck to create the feeling of pressure. He gulps as it touches him and presses his hands into the floor, fingertips cadaver-white aside from the nicotine stains.

Daniel is at the flip chart, writing it all down, careful to inscribe Nigel's own words. Frank is playing Nigel. From my position on the floor, I sneak a quick scan around the room, bringing my own self back to reality and away from the dying Kelly. Wayne is sitting with his head in his hands, rocking. Jeremy sits bolt upright, staring at me. Kyle is looking out of the window, lips pursed. Daniel nods at me. We all look at Nigel on the floor, corpse-like. Eyes still clenched.

We elicit some more thoughts and feelings from Nigel about how the offence may have felt from Kelly's point of view. 'Terrible', 'disgusting', 'scared'. He is limited in his repertoire of emotions but seems genuinely affected by the experience. The room is as still as a funeral parlour. It is the first offence re-enactment I have directed, and I cannot believe how powerful it feels. I know it is Nigel lying like a dumped sack on the floor in the group room and yet it feels like it is Kelly. Somehow, we have created a glimpse into the real offence right there in the room.

'OK, Kelly, we are going to leave it there,' I say. 'Come and sit on this chair for me.'

Nigel lies there for some time. Everyone sits in silence and Kyle continues to stare out of the window. Frank is looking anxious.

'Are you …' he starts to ask of Nigel.

I raise my eyebrows, glaring at him, and press my finger to my lips, trying to communicate that Nigel is staying in role as his victim for now. Nigel pulls himself up, crawls to the chair and shudders, as if he is trying to shake off a second skin. We debrief him in role as Kelly and ask him how he feels. Nigel does not seem able to speak.

'Horrible,' he croaks.

'OK, now let's de-role you. Come and move into this chair for me, where you will be back in the room as Nigel. Group, can you ask him some questions to help him de-role, please?' I say.

They like this bit. The pressure is off for five minutes.

'What did you have for breakfast, Nige, mate?'

'What's your middle name, Nigel?'

A few questions later and we have established that Nigel is out of role and back in the room as himself. We ask him what he has learnt from the role-play.

'I can't believe how long a minute is,' he sighs eventually.

Previously, when we had asked about how long the sexual assault was on his victim, he had replied, in a throwaway tone, 'only about a minute'. I timed it to the second in the role play. It had felt like ten.

'It must have … felt like a very long time … to her,' he says.

We revisit some of the CDs he held about the victim – 'able to leave if she wanted to' and 'wanted to be there with me'. Nigel is now able to revise his view of how his victim may have been thinking and feeling at the time. She could not leave. She did not really want to be there. She did not 'need teaching about sex'. We are chipping away at his beliefs and his personal construction of the offence that somehow the victim played an active role. He looks worn out. Gravestone-grey and still shaking. He cannot give us eye contact. Nigel's offence, the sexual assault and murder of a thirteen-year-old child, always causes the group to baulk and to give him a hard time in the group exercises. However, they sit in tentative awe of him today.

'Time for a tea break?' says Frank, trying to rescue us all again.

We are on victim empathy re-enactments and role plays. It is the part of the group that we have all been dreading. It is tough, with so much to remember and get right. It is also uncomfortable and awkward, running through a graphic description of a sexual offence and directing the re-enactment of it with the prisoner in role as his victim. Daniel, Len and I will take it in turns to be the role-play director. Daniel, Len or one of the other prisoners will have to play the perpetrator in the replayed scene, repeating the language and actions as they happened, although 'the perpetrator' does not touch 'the victim' or use any props. That's the job of the role-play director.

After yet more weak tea out of a scabby plastic cup, it is Wayne's turn. Daniel is leading this one. He leads Wayne through getting into role as one of his rape victims and sets the scene – in the front room, lights low, TV on – covering the time of day and her expectations about the evening. It makes me remember that evening in my own home when I had visions of a masked, armed rapist hiding behind the sofa. I can feel a prickle as the hairs on my neck react to my apprehension. It runs up towards my ears, like a scurrying spider, and makes me shiver. We have turned the lights off, which only emphasises the glum atmosphere we are creating. The faces of the other men around the edges of the room are blurred in the gloom of the drizzly late-summer afternoon. I feel uneasy about them when they are lurking in the shadows. They have become monsters again in the dark. I am relieved Daniel is here.

Daniel runs through the re-enactment. He uses a ruler as a prop for a knife and, sitting Wayne on the floor, binds his hands together with bandages. It becomes clear once Wayne's hands are tied that something is wrong. He is leaning forward, rocking and trying to get into a foetal position. I shake my head at Daniel, alarmed. This does not feel right.

'Do you want a time-out?' asks Daniel, reacting to me, our physical intimacy on hold but our emotional connection an advantage when facilitating together.

Wayne nods. His lips are as white as bone and he is in torpor. He cannot explain his distress. I do not know what to do, aside from reassure him that he is back in the room. We stop the role play and Wayne recovers in his chair as we bring him out of role and end the session with more weak tea. The group is stunned by his reaction, offering him a smoke and wanting to know that he is OK. I am out of my depth. I am the psychologist here. What the hell is going on? I know it is a reaction to something. Is Wayne reliving his own childhood trauma? Have we triggered something by the binding of his hands? This did not happen in the training. My instincts are to make him feel safe and not to push it. He seems to have come round by the time he leaves the group room, but I ring the wing and ask the member of staff answering the phone to keep an eye on him. I get a grunt in response.

In our debrief we discuss whether Wayne may have been sexually abused as a child but feels unable to disclose. He keeps hinting at it and his fear and dislike of women is strong. Childhood trauma and abuse of the men is given no weight in the SOTP, and HM Prison Service do not provide counselling for the men for their own abuse. This is partly as historical sexual abuse is not considered a dynamic and treatable risk factor (there is no evidence that addressing it will reduce risk), so it does not justify the resources. Prison is about punishment, not privileged personal therapy. The men are there to address their offending, not their own victimisation, and we are not given the time, space or skills to deal with it. It feels like this part of their history is not important and their experiences as children are not relevant to their offending. I instinctively know that this cannot be right for those who have been abused. They were all young, vulnerable, innocent children once too. Some of them victims themselves. Do we not owe them any validation or compassion?

CHAPTER ELEVEN

VICTIM EMPATHY
ROLE PLAYS

On a damp autumnal morning, Andy sits hunched in his chair as he does every session, huge hands crossed over his huge stomach, occasionally twiddling and inspecting his thumbs.

'It's your turn today, Andy, and we are going to re-enact the offence with Jessie, your niece. We know there were two victims, but we are going to concentrate on Jessie today. How are you feeling about it?' I say.

He shrugs his bulky shoulders in response.

I bring him over to the empty chair that we have placed in the middle of the room. Len is scribing today, more comfortable in this role than the complex one I am undertaking. I wish Daniel were here for back-up.

'When you sit in this chair you are taking on the role of Jessie, your ten-year-old niece,' I say to Andy.

He nods and sits down, pressing his hands back in position over his stomach like a protective stab vest.

I put him in role as best I can, trying to help the resistant, bearded, twenty-stone man in front of me adopt the mind of a ten-year-old girl: her age, what she looks like, what she enjoys doing at school.

I lie 'Jessie' on the floor and 'put her' into the scene of the offence, asking what she can see, hear, smell, how she feels and what she is wearing *as the victim*.

'I'm in bed with my pink furry blanket and teddies. I've got my nightie on. I can smell my Uncle Andy's breath. It smells funny.'

The room is perfectly still. The rain slaps the windows.

In a soft voice, as if talking to a real child, I ask, 'What are you thinking? What are you feeling? What can you see? What do you want to happen?'

I think I can see a faint tremor in Andy's bearded chin, but he answers the questions. 'She' is scared of this huge smelly man. 'She' is feeling sick and wants to scream but is too frightened. Her arms and legs have stopped working. 'She' does not like this sort of tickling and wants it to stop.

I take 'Jessie' through what happened to her at the hands of Andy, and I ask, 'Are you going to tell your dad, Jessie?'

'Yeah,' comes a small voice.

I move 'Jessie' into a chair for the debrief.

'Well, Jessie, you do tell your dad, and he thinks it's a joke,' I say. 'Tell us what you are thinking now.'

Andy/Jessie moves his meaty hands off his stomach so that they swing by his sides.

'Sad and scared that he doesn't believe me, and that it will happen again.'

Andy/Jessie lets out a sigh and puts his hands over his face. He does not move, and I let it run. Silence is a powerful tool. I will Frank, forever in rescue mode, to stay quiet for once. Eventually Andy fills the gap.

'This is fuckin' awful. Can we stop now?'

I am surprised, yet pleased, that the role play has had such an impact on him. Running through the sexual assault of a small child in bed has taken its toll on me, though. I need there to be a benefit.

'What I want to know, Andy,' says Jeremy grand-iosely, in interview mode after we have de-roled Andy, 'is this.' He pauses for effect. 'Was it really "just once"?'

There is more tense silence, which the whole room, even Frank, knows not to fill.

Andy shakes his head. 'Was more than once, but once is enough, too much. Don't wanna talk about it. Can we have a break?'

'We can have a break, Andy, but can we stay with this for another minute? I think you are saying that the abuse happened more than once, is that right? That is different from what you have been saying all along,' I say.

Len has his mouth open, pen poised in mid-air at this breakthrough.

Andy nodded. 'It happened lots of times, like she said. And her sister too. Can we have a break now?'

'Yes, we can, and well done for being honest, Andy. How does that feel?'

That is one step too far. He shrugs his shoulders. Jeremy seeks my gaze and gives me a smug grin and a self-satisfied nod. I can imagine him saying to himself, 'See? Look at me, that confession is all my work. I am better than you at this with my superior skills and life experience.'

I need to have some supervision about him, I think. The sanctimonious git. He is getting right under my skin.

Len and I take our debrief to the smoke room. We need to be out of the group room. Bronwyn is already there, laughing so much she is crying, black mascara running down her freckled cheeks. I can just see her through the swirling ochre smoke of the little cell-come-smoking room located in a dingy corner of the department. Cigarette in hand, she regales the gathered SOTP facilitators with her story.

'So, there's me and Kenny practising our re-enactment this morning before the group, when he bends over to do the leg-prodding bit and his trousers split! No joke, straight up the arse. You could see his pants.' She wipes the tears from her eyes. 'Take over, Kenny, I can't speak.'

'Then,' says Kenny, her officer co-facilitator, smiling as usual, 'we have to get the stapler out in the group room, and I have to staple them up, like, before the group comes in and sees me without me kegs on!'

Bronwyn is howling. She sponges her eyes again with the arm of her suit jacket and replaces her glasses. 'Then we have to run the whole re-enactment for real with the men, with his trousers stapled!'

'Yeah,' says Kenny. 'Thought they were gonna split again as I leaned in with the old marker pen, but they held tight.'

'I couldn't look!' squeaks Bronwyn.

We are all laughing by now. Kenny is taking it all in good humour, eyes shining, and loving the attention. More cigarettes are passed round between the eight or nine of us regulars squeezed in there, and I share what happened with Andy.

'He finally admitted it!' I say, smiling at Daniel, who has appeared for the debrief and is drawing hard on his menthol cigarette before passing it on to me. This inner circle of colleagues know about us now.

'And he says it happened more than once.'

'Result. Well done, you two. See? Those role plays do work,' he says with a nod to Len, who soaks up the praise and grins at me before returning to his nail-chewing and smoking, somehow achieving both activities in parallel.

There is a knock on the door. We are safe from the Axe Murderer in here. She does not dare venture in. The stream of smoke emitting from underneath the door, the guffaws of the gaggle of officers in uniform and the content of our winding-down-from-group conversations are enough to keep her tucked away in her office.

It is Louise. She seeks me out through the haze. Do I want some supervision about Jeremy? She does not come in either but understands and accepts that this is where the real debrief to the gruelling work we are doing happens. Where we use gallows humour, as it's known, to deflate, dehumanise and detach from the distressing material we are all being exposed to. It brings us all closer together and normalises what we are hearing. Never do we intend to disrespect victims or offences; we are just trying to cope and make sense of it as best we can.

Nobody seems shocked anymore at what we hear on the SOTP. There are no limits to the debauched violence, horror and humiliation that human beings inflict on one another. I am scared I am becoming immune. I hear myself describe offences as 'just one rape' or 'a straight-forward murder'. And then comes a rush of feeling guilty that I can even think like that: I sound like one of the prisoners before an active account session. I hear the other facilitators do it too. Of course, there is no such thing as 'just a straight murder', but my baseline has moved permanently. We are working with the most complex, high-risk sexual offenders in the prison system, and we deal with it with poor humour, mocking banter and chain-smoking in a cramped, foggy cell where we can barely see each other's faces but, thankfully, can hear each other laugh.

I leave to the sound of Kenny retelling his story accompanied by more shrieks of laughter from Bronwyn. I smile. This makes it all worthwhile. The long days in a dirty, dangerous world with limited daylight. The grisly information we must extract in detail, like a sharp splinter stuck in a festering wound. And the constant dull nag, like toothache, that I could always be the next victim if I do not watch my back. It is these hard-working, loyal and funny colleagues, who are always ready to listen if you need it but are far more likely to give you a fag and take the piss, that get me through the day. I feel like I am developing a second head. One for prison working and one for the rest of my life.

CHAPTER TWELVE

IMPOSTER SYNDROME

Daniel and I are returning from a session one day after a role play and heading to the smoke-room debrief to be greeted by Maxine striding down the corridor towards us.

'Rebecca. A word. On your own. In my office,' she barks.

There is no option to refuse, so I follow the diminutive Axe Murderer into her cell.

'I have become aware that you are in a relationship with Daniel,' she says. Only her lip-glossed mouth moves. 'I am really disappointed, Rebecca. I thought better of you. You can't mix sex and sex-offender treatment. You are playing with fire, you silly girl. This is not a game.'

I feel like a small child and want to cry. Her judgemental, disapproving tone takes me straight back to being told off by my mother. The secret is out. She knows. Everyone knows. Even his wife knows, as I found out this week when I answered the home phone to her justified anger and tears. There are no official consequences – we are free, consenting adults – but the gloss of the hidden affair has tarnished, like an old silver trophy in need of a polish. It does not feel quite as exciting anymore. More like I have got myself tangled up in something really stupid and difficult. I'm starting to see that, despite the passion, he is manipulative and selfish, playing his wife and me off against each other. Keeping us both on the hook, swinging.

In addition to the re-enactments, we also run bespoke role plays, which are designed to enhance the men's awareness of their victims' experiences. We consider how parents, siblings and friends of the immediate victim might have been affected. These are not in the form of re-enacting a known scene, but scenarios designed to tap into other perspectives to try to address any deficits in their understanding of the consequences of their crimes. Each prisoner does a re-enactment, and then a couple of bespoke role plays.

One role play we design for Frank is to consider the impact on the young policewoman who found his victim's body in the shallow hole he dug in his back garden. We put him into role as the policewoman and take him through the discovery, as if she were being interviewed about it. He freewheels in role. He does not know how the policewoman might have felt, and neither

do we, but we are trying to introduce him to the possibil-
ities. How finding the body might have affected her
work, her life at home, with her boyfriend or family. He
is stilted and finds it difficult, but he tries his best. He
considers his answers, and it is almost like I can see the
neurons starting to fire in his brain, making new connections.

He shakes his head as I bring him out of role.

'That's hard, Miss. I never loiked the poi-lice, but it
must have been hard for her all roight.'

Back in the group room the following day, Jeremy is
next for his role-play sessions. He sits there eyeing us
with a wad of prepared notes on his knee.

'I am not sure who will be "dealing"' – he lifts his
fingers into inverted commas – 'with me. Probably you,
Daniel, as I know you have run groups before.'

I can feel the warm flood of blood to my neck, cheeks
and ears. He is right, but how can he, I think to myself,
be so condescending and pompous? He is a bloody
murderer and rapist. How can he make me feel so small,
unworthy and unskilled? I sit up taller, as if to match
him, although I feel tiny and insignificant.

'I have an idea,' he goes on. 'I think it will be best,
Daniel, if you put me in the role of the police officer
discovering my victim's body. I have given it some
thought. Given my experience on the force, and my life
experience, of course, I think I can do a really good job.'

He looks at Daniel. The cowlick is really misbehaving today and despite Jeremy's obvious best attempts to flatten it with God knows what, it has a life of its own and is waving around like a sapling in a storm. That must really piss him off every day, I think, smiling to myself. It's so at odds with the rest of his carefully controlled appearance.

Thankfully Daniel answers. Jeremy has me crushed at that moment, beaten in the psychological battle we are in, and he knows it. Some days I feel so skilled in the group, but on others he strips me back to an unsure young trainee, not long out of university.

'Thanks for that, Jeremy. Good to see you have been thinking about it, but we don't think that will be the best role play for you. We are trying to think about perspectives that you've *not* thought of before,' Daniel says.

'Oh, I see,' says Jeremy, his notes slithering to the floor. 'If that's what you think, Daniel, I trust in your experience.'

'And Rebecca will be leading on this; we all have the same skills and training.'

'I would have expected her to have more,' says Jeremy. 'She is *supposed* to be a psychologist. She should have a degree, like me.'

'Don't worry, Jeremy, I have a degree, *and* I've just finished a master's degree, actually,' I say, clawing back some ground and giving him a triumphant little smile.

'Well, we'd better get on with it then,' says Jeremy, trying to keep the upper hand. 'What have you got planned for me?'

I grit my teeth. 'We are going to start with a re-enactment of the rape of your victim,' I say. 'We think it will be really useful for you to try to identify some of the specific emotions she may have been experiencing.'

'Whatever you say. You are the experts, after all,' he says with a slight nod, staring at Daniel.

Later, after the session, I meet with Louise in her office to have my supervision.

'How did it go with Jeremy's re-enactment?' she asks, leaning in, slender fingers pushing back her long frizzy hair.

On a practical level, the re-enactment was a success. I remembered everything when I should have done – the chronology of the offence, what the victim said and what the perpetrator did – just as we had planned. Jeremy had reeled off several emotions in the debrief, as if he had been consulting a dictionary, yet there was no depth of feeling and no physical reaction from him. It is as if he is impenetrable, like a stone sponge, and the re-enactment washed over him. Cognitively he 'gets it' – he can list the consequences – but according to our training, that is not our only aim. We want an emotional connection.

'Sounds like you did a good job,' reassures Louise, 'but I am interested in the effect on you.'

I do not point out that Professor Bunting said, 'Everything before the but is bullshit.' I explain how I felt as we started the session. That he was pushing my buttons and I felt deskilled.

'I don't know why he does that to me,' I say.

'Sounds like good old imposter syndrome rearing its head,' says Louise. 'You are really good at what you do. But it seems very common in female psychologists.'

I ignore the 'but' again and allow myself a little glow inside. I respect Louise and her opinion. We talk through some techniques to handle Jeremy. Louise thinks we are like a pair of piano stools, each trying to reach a higher elevation than the other. 'Try to stop spinning yours,' she says. 'Remember, *you* are the psychologist, not him.'

I am not sure it always feels like that, but I keep it to myself.

'And how is it running the group with your … er … new … partner?' she says.

I knew this spiky issue had been on the way.

'It's OK. We try to keep it all separate – you know, the group and … er … everything else.'

I talk openly about sex, every day, with several sex offenders, but I am struggling with this conversation about my own life.

'Well, it must be difficult. Unusual. So please be careful. Are you sure the group don't know?' she says.

I am pretty sure, but they are clever and experts at deception, and I wouldn't put it past Jeremy to work it out, despite his lack of emotional intelligence. I do not like the deceit either. We are unearthing their secrets and it all feels a little hypocritical. I feel as duplicitous as them.

Daniel and I do not talk openly about the impact the group has on our relationship. Our affair is very physical, exciting and passionate, and I am relieved at the lack of intrusion of the offences on our personal life, despite my worry. We are complete professionals at work. It would be impossible to slide into any intimacy with each other after running a role play. I always feel dirty and drained and like I need to escape the room. But the work follows us home. We talk about the men, their characters, strategies we can try and role plays we can design while watching the TV at my house on the nights he leaves his wife and stays over with me. It is hard not to. The group is all-consuming and takes so much energy and many hours of our lives.

One evening in bed I make a harmless remark, and Daniel loses it.

'I'm sorry, I can't – that just took me straight back to what Jessie, Andy's victim, said,' he says.

He looks mortified and we get dressed in silence.

I also have the occasional intrusive thought, triggered by something Daniel says or does, but I manage to deal with it. We attempt to keep it all very detached and my two heads come in handy yet again. We try our very best to keep the group and the sex offences out of our relationship, but it's tricky. I believe the relationship did not have an impact on the job, but despite our best efforts, the job did have an impact on the relationship.

The last re-enactment is with Kyle. None of us has been looking forward to this. He sits in his favourite chair. Legs splayed. Arms crossed.

'How are you feeling about today, Kyle?' asks Daniel.

'Special!' answers Kyle

'Oh, why's that?'

'Well, there's three of you here today – that's not normal. Is that cos I'm just too much to handle?'

He winks at me. Daniel spots him.

'Why are you winking at Rebecca?'

'Keep your hair on, mate, just a joke. Let's get it over with.'

'Well, you wouldn't wink at anyone else in here, so don't wink at her, all right?'

'Bit protective, aren't you, Dan? What's so special about her?'

'Well, I'm leading today so come over here onto Jade's chair and we'll put you in role.'

'I was hoping Rebecca would do it.'

'Really? Why's that?' Daniel asks.

'With her being the psychologist and all, with my case, I think I need the expert.'

Jeremy gives a huff.

'We are a team, as you well know. Now come and sit over here, please,' Daniel says through tight lips.

Daniel tries to put Kyle into role.

'What are you wearing, Jade?'

'A reaaallly short skirt.'

'What do you look like?'

'Really attractive, big breasts.'

He looks at me and smirks. He is enjoying this, I think. I wonder if we should stop. I try to catch Daniel's eye, but he isn't looking. Frank has his hand over his mouth like he is trying to stop words dropping out.

Daniel carries on and asks what 'Jade' is expecting from the evening.

'I'm hoping for sex.'

Len is writing it all up on the board and I see him give a tiny shake of his head. Wayne is noticeably shaking his head.

Daniel runs through the offence according to the depositions – the violence, the sexual assaults, the stripping of the victim's clothes and the urination. Kyle lies on the floor with his hands resting on his chest, fingers entwined like he is going to drop into a pleasant snooze. He answers the questions he is asked: how are you feeling? What are you thinking, Jade?

'Horrible, terrible, horrible, bad, awful,' come the list of rote emotions.

Daniel goes to drip water onto Kyle, to signify him urinating on his victim.

Kyle splutters and laughs out loud. I look at Daniel.

'OK, I think we need to stop here,' I say.

Kyle leaps up off the floor.

'Well, that's a damn shame, I was really getting into that.'

He pushes his hand against his genitals. Does he have an erection? Have the rape and the violence we have tried to re-enact just sexually aroused him? Should I say something? The moment passes, so I let it go. I realise I am too scared of Kyle to say anything. Kyle reclines in his chair and lights a pre-rolled cigarette, blowing the smoke out in a leisurely way towards the ceiling in little puffs.

'You are not taking this seriously, man,' says Wayne, shaking his head again. 'You shunt be 'ere. You're taking the piss.'

'Just doing what I've been told on my Sentence Plan,' says Kyle, examining the tip of his cigarette.

'Yes. We know your game,' says Jeremy. 'You're only doing this group to get your parole.'

'Aren't we all?' says Kyle.

'Well, I'm certainly not,' says Jeremy, curling his lip.

'Me neither,' say Wayne and Frank in unison.

Nigel sits silently and Andy tuts and shakes his giant head.

* * *

'I've had enough of that cocky little twat,' says Daniel when we debrief. 'He doesn't give a shit. He's here for all the wrong reasons. And he's got a thing for you.'

Len nods.

'Do you think he was aroused, you know, in the role play?' I say.

Daniel looks at me, eyebrows raised. 'Really? Wish I'd noticed that. Wouldn't be surprised, though. He doesn't regret raping and battering that poor girl for one second,' he says.

Len shakes his head.

'I'm always worried about you in there with him. I feel like I've always got to be watching him in case he tries to get hold of you or something. I'm glad these role plays are over – you can keep away from them all now,' says Daniel.

'At least we know what we are up against with Kyle; I know he is dangerous. Let's hope the Parole Board can see it too,' I say.

'You can't polish a turd,' declares Len.

The victim empathy block has left us exhausted. There is so much to remember on a practical level: the order of getting into and out of role, the details and chronology of the offence. They also drain us of all emotion, and I always feel empty afterwards. Yet the role playing seems to be having an impact, and, as I keep reminding Len in the debriefs, that is exactly why we are here. It is hard to explain the immense power of the role plays, especially the re-enactments and the accompanying heavy silence that flattens the room as if we are in some peculiar vacuum. How we are never assaulted, how we manage not to laugh and how we do not cry. How we justify flicking water on them as proxy ejaculate, wrap bandages around their eyes as blindfolds, or around their ankles or hands as binds, mimicking what they did to their victims. How they do not get erections as a young female psychologist, who must smell like fresh candy floss and pure sex after years of incarceration, ties them up on the floor, leans close and prods a pen dangerously close to their groin. Or maybe they do. I must get in so close to the men to do my job. In some role plays I am crouched right beside them and can see and feel them breathing. I am acutely aware of being female in these situations.

Over various groups, some of them cry and some of them do not. There are some genuine tears for themselves, their victims and the realisation of lives ruined. Others are manipulative crocodile tears, put on for show as they think that is what we will want to see. Screwed-up faces, hands over eyes and loud sobs, but no actual wetness. We always discuss their tears, trying to probe what is going on: Who are you crying for? What are you crying about? What has particularly upset you? We try to be alert to behavioural leaks – the body telling us that what is coming out of their mouths may not be genuine.

A lack of eye contact or a searching about in the air with their gaze as if the answer lies on the ceiling, facial expressions that don't fit the story or stay too long etched on the face, a scratch of the nose or ear at a key question, foot-tapping or leg-twitching, finger-picking, nail-biting. We *think* we can tell who is genuine and who is not. We *think* we know the men at this stage of the treatment and are not to be fooled. But – I've noted the 'but' – only they ever know if there is a shift inside.

I would later work with a quirky, pasty-faced young man with an impressive mop of hair the colour of a daffodil. In the group he discusses at length the singular rape and hammer attack he has been convicted of and appears dedicated to not doing it again. He is insightful in his active account and appears affected by the re-enactment and role plays, and although not particularly emotional, he says and does all the things that make him believable. We write him a positive treatment report and then move on to the next group, counting him as a success.

Years later I am watching the BBC's *News at Ten* and he appears, older and more pallid and being escorted from court after being handed three life sentences. I know it is him, as there is no mistaking the pallor and bright yellow hair. He has been charged and convicted – while still in prison – of several historical rapes and violent assaults and the murder of a young woman using a claw hammer. I know he must have given us a false life story in the group and lied his way through it. I am stunned that we did not spot it. We spent over 200 intensive hours with him over the best part of a year, pushing and poking around in his history. I never once suspected the sustained years of his offending, or that he had committed a murder. He was clever, determined and manipulative, and he conned us. The whole oddball presentation kept people at a distance, and we underestimated him.

I am quickly over the shock. This is the nature of the individuals we work with. However, I am surprised by the skill with which he deceived us all, including the other prisoners who, by default, are the real authorities on murder and rape. It makes me wonder how many more of them have tricked us and said what we wanted to hear. Despite all the successful books and theories on understanding body language – and the field has developed considerably since – I think it is tricky to catch out a motivated and intelligent liar.

Working with one notorious serial child killer in another group, who scored highly on psychopathy, I suspected there were many more murder/sexual assault victims, and the police did too. He had steely blue eyes, like marbles that had been in the freezer, a dry sense of humour and a peculiar, almost sweet, musty smell. He sat on the SOTP for months, and, aside from cracking the odd joke, was unyielding, like a sealed clam. He clearly liked the tea and biscuits, and possibly the company and listening to the other offences. He also told us he liked children in white socks, but apart from that we did not get very far with him, and it all seemed a bit pointless. He took his well-guarded secrets to his uncelebrated grave. This felt so cruel to the families living in limbo. I was hoping to 'crack' him, and there would have been a certain status to this, but he was an obstinate man, and Clarice Starling I am not. In my experience, real-life serial killers are far less exciting and much more stubborn and smelly than those portrayed in the films.

CHAPTER THIRTEEN

GROUP END

'Custard cream or chocolate digestive?' I say, handing the plate of biscuits to Wayne. 'We've also got fig rolls – who asked for those?'

It is the last session of the group. Daniel, Len and I have put in our own money and bought a dizzying array of treats for the men. They have requested items that they cannot order on their 'canteen'. Food that they have not had in years but that we all take for granted, like Monster Munch pickled onion flavour crisps. It is like a scene from an office Christmas party, but without the paper hats and wine. We are enhancing our Care Bear stereotype even further, but we are past worrying. The group is at an end. We will not ever meet again, and it feels like the termination of something important for us all. We have spent around 200 hours in this smelly, tired group room with the men sharing the most intimate details of their lives.

I am convinced that we have made a difference, at least to some of them. Wayne and Frank have come a long way in understanding their offences, their CDs and the impact on their victims. In the 'relapse prevention' sessions we have just finished, they both voiced over and over how determined they are not to commit more offences, listing various risk factors – thoughts, feelings, behaviours and situations – as red flags to avoid, control and escape (the ACE system). Despite their issues with spelling, they have copied them out onto little index cards we have provided. I notice Frank has his ACE cards tucked in the top pocket of his freshly ironed shirt. They have both shown their vulnerabilities in the group and appear genuinely affected by the victim empathy sessions.

I note how Wayne has stopped showing his self-harm scars and now wears a smart striped prison shirt with long sleeves in place of his tatty blue T-shirt. He has combed his hair. It is as if he is taking more pride in himself and going to lengths to fix himself, both internally and externally. I still do not know what trauma happened to him as a child that caused him to grow up into such a damaged man. And why does finding out fascinate me? I realise I still need to understand. I don't feel like I have the full picture. There must be more to this than just getting a confession that matches the deps.

Frank looks like he is having the time of his life at a real party. He has piles of biscuits stacked on each knee and is grinning. I am still troubled by those pictures of his victim in her crude grave and the thought of him digging away and hanging curtains at the windows. As with Wayne, I still think we need to know more about why. Why did he take it that far? Lots of men must get in situations where someone has refused them sex, for whatever reason. They don't rape and kill the person and bury them in the garden. Why is Frank different?

Andy is making the most of the food too and looks the most content I have ever seen him. He has also made some treatment gains, perhaps tipped into progress by his admissions in the victim empathy sessions. However, he does not appear to have the motivation, the hunger or perhaps desperation to change like Frank and Wayne. He is rather dismissive of the relapse prevention sessions, stating that his offences are such a long time ago that he need not identify any risk factors. He remains focused on the murder as the 'real' offending.

Nigel has taken only one biscuit and sits nibbling on it with his protruding teeth, like a hungry mouse. He still has a way to go. His negative thoughts about himself and his sexual interest in girls are all too entrenched. Will we ever know why some men grow up like this? What has caused him to develop such interests? Was he born like this? Will those interests be there forever? He has managed to stay in the group, despite the obvious dislike of him and his offences by the others. I am not sure he will ever be released, at least not until he is a very old man.

Angry young Kyle is still angry and still young. He had been first in line to take just as much of the party food as he wanted, and nobody challenged him. The group has been an eventful journey for him. He has admitted to new parts of his offending; however, I can't help but wonder if this has all been part of some master plan – to make it look like he has been making progress in an attempt to sway the Parole Board. I cannot forget his remorseless and disturbing behaviour in the role plays. I am convinced he was aroused by the rape re-enactment. We have discussed with Louise whether he is a sadist – taking pleasure in the pain of others – and we reasoned that it's possible. He used more violence than was necessary to force his victim into compliance: she would have probably done anything asked of her in that moment and he enjoyed her distress. He committed the extreme violence and humiliation alongside the rape because he liked it and it aroused him. There isn't much evidence from the rest of his life that this is a pattern, but we haven't managed to explore his fantasy in any depth. We know that he tortured his dog and this fits with our suspicions. I think he is selfish, impulsive, deviant and dangerous, and will need to mature and change considerably before any consideration of release. I also believe that he is entirely capable of doing it again and that the group work will have minimal impact.

Jeremy sits there with a paper towel neatly placed on his jeans to catch the crumbs. He is smiling, which is a rare sight. My thoughts about him are mixed. We have a difficult relationship. I am learning through my personal therapy sessions with the insightful and patient counsellor (each facilitator must have three mandatory sessions during an SOTP group) that his attitude trips me into feeling inadequate. Feeling not good enough stems from my embedded view of myself that if I had been good enough, my mother would not have left. Boxes are shifting in my warehouse, but they are heavy and awkward, and it all feels very raw. With my head I can see it and say that I am good enough. In my heart I cannot feel it or believe it. The counsellor says I must work on connecting my head and my heart. Jeremy would have fallen off his chair at that, but I can understand what she means. It is going to take some working on, just like Jeremy and his issues.

Nevertheless, I can see that Jeremy has made progress in shifting some of his boxes too. He has spent hours doing colour-coded, laminated ACE cards and has shown them to us with pride. However, he still sees himself as superior to everyone – including the facilitators – despite his offences. It is as if he cannot quite align himself with what he has done. The offence is a blip in his otherwise unblemished and successful life. Perhaps this is a protection system for him, as is the need to still see himself as a police officer. He still has an identity to hold onto and one that is opposed to offending. He cannot seem to reconcile the two contrasting characters. Jeremy is barren of emotion and we have not managed to make any inroads with this during treatment. What has happened to him to cause such a shut-off? He too has a long way to go, although I do not think it will or should be me that can help him on his journey. I think we press each other's buttons a little too hard and a little too often.

Working with the men has strengthened my belief that people can change if they want to, no matter how they have behaved in the past. I had not expected to enjoy the group as much as I have. It has been all-encompassing for the last ten months, and I have been immersed in their lives, stories and offences. I have coped with hearing the offences and genuinely grown to like some of them as people, seeing beyond what they have done. Despite their crimes, I do not see them as monsters. More than once I have noticed that I had thought or behaved in the same way as one of them. I have seen that the attitudes some of them hold, particularly about women and sex, are no different from those of certain wing officers. The difference in the group is that some of these men are starting to recognise such beliefs as potentially dangerous, disrespectful and inappropriate, and are trying to do something about it. I still feel very inexperienced and exposed during the sessions, although I have grown in my skills and confidence. I am still wearing high-necked tops.

* * *

In that last session, with the fresh spring sunshine trying to break through the grimy barred windows like a perfectly timed metaphor, we do a final round robin. Out of character, Andy goes first.

'It's been OK,' he says with a grin, hands pinned across his belly. 'I've enjoyed the biscuits.'

He is using humour to deflect, as he normally does, but we praise him for his progress and move on.

Nigel is second, not by choice, but because we are heading in that direction round the room now.

'It has been really tough and really hard for me, but I have learnt a lot about what I put my victim through,' he says, staring at the floor.

'You've done all roight, Nige,' says Frank, and Nigel raises his head and gives an unusually wide smile.

Wayne says, 'It's bin awful, but it's changed me so much. I understand me much better. Thanks to you all.'

He nods and smiles at us. I smile back and we heap on the praise for the progress he has made in taking responsibility for his behaviour.

'Yes, Wayne, you have done really rather well. Good for you,' says Jeremy, which is a bit of a surprise to us all.

Frank is desperate for it to be his turn, edging forward in his chair and almost dropping his stack of biscuits.

'I know what Rebecca's favourite car is! And I will never forget all you facilitators, thanks. You're bostin' and I will never do anything like this ever again.'

I really hope not, Frank, I think. Please don't let me down. I feel like I have invested so much in this newly motivated and excitable man.

Kyle, leaning back in his chair with face set on 'cannot care less', says, 'Been good to get out of my cell every day and not have to go to work like the rest of the numb-skulls in this jail.'

He flashes a grin at me. 'And to see Rebecca every week – she's far better looking than the shop instructors.'

To my surprise it is Jeremy who speaks.

'Shouldn't have bothered coming then,' he sneers. 'If that's all you can say after ten months, it's pathetic. Really pathetic.'

After what seemed like a defence of me, Jeremy flips into his usual mode.

'Well, as it's my turn, and we are all being honest, I was hoping to learn a bit more from the group really. Hoping to really understand my psyche. I think perhaps I will do a psychology degree after my history degree. How hard can it be? Should be interesting.'

He flashes me a little smile and I can see his straight white teeth. They look like a row of war graves. I tell him I find psychology interesting too. In response to my supervision sessions, I am trying not to bite, respond or battle with him. I am the psychologist, not him, I remind myself. Keep the piano stool still.

They all file out for the last time, Cat-A books signed, and pockets loaded with biscuits. Every one of them says 'thanks', even Kyle. Frank offers me his hand on the way out. This is a new boundary to be broken. I have never touched a prisoner, skin to skin, only ever from the end of a marker pen. It is an unspoken golden rule that there is no physical contact between us. Our eyes meet.

'Thanks ever so much, Miss,' he says, in his strong Brummie accent. 'Thanks for changing moi loife.'

I shake his clammy hand.

'Good luck, Frank, and don't let me down,' I say.

'I won't, Miss. Never, Miss,' he says.

Louise comes to see us for our final debrief and, head therapeutically tilted, asks us how we are all feeling.

'Glad it's ov'er,' says Len, munching his way through the solitary remaining jammie dodger. 'Can't go through that again, working on't wings is easier.'

'I understand,' says Louise, 'but thank you for your work. Hopefully between you all you have made a difference for future victims.' We let the words sink in. This is why we are here, after all.

'It's just we'll never know them,' says Len, back to chewing his fingernails. 'Only time us lot'll find out is if one of them does it again. I've enjoyed working with you two, mind.' He turns to Daniel and me. 'You're cut out for it, the both of you, but it's not for me na more.'

'I'm sorry to hear that, Len,' Louise says. 'Is there something that's bothering you?'

'Aye … it's just hearing all them offences all the time. I can't get them out of my head, like I've said before. And there's sommat else – I've been talking to the counsellor about it 'n' all, but I don't mind telling you lot.'

He sighs. 'I'm always looking where I've got me hands, like, on the nippers at home. I can't bath the little lass anymore. The wife's gotta do it. And I used to love bath time with them nippers. And putting them to bed. I can't do that neither. Counsellor has said it'll be reet, it's normal, but nowt feels normal no more. I'm seeing things differently now. Me wife says so. It's all that deviant stuff. I can't get it out me head, like.'

'I'm so sorry, Len,' I say.

'Aye, lass, 'tis what it is. Seen all sorts in my time, but nowt like this. Just not cut out for it, I guess. I'll go back on't wings. But I hope you lot carry on. Someone's got to do it.'

Poor Len, who has given everything he can to queen and country, and a roomful of convicted sex offenders too. I've also noticed that I have started to look at the world differently. If I see a man with a child, I am more conscious of it: Has he kidnapped her? Where is he touching her? Why is he buying her sweets? The other day I found myself following an old man, who was shopping with a little girl, around the supermarket, keeping one eye on how he was interacting with her as I pretended to look at the cornflakes. He was no doubt her doting granddad, but my outlook feels altered now. As if I am on high alert for danger like an oversensitive smoke alarm, permanently set to notice the way every man deals with every child.

'Yeah, it changes you, the SOTP,' I agree.

Daniel nods. 'It does, but we've got to do this job, haven't we? How else are we going to stop them? I think it suits some of us more than others and affects us all in different ways. I saw the knife sticking straight up out of the butter the other day and it did my head in.'

'What's the relevance of that?' asks Louise.

'Well, on my first SOTP I dealt with a man who stabbed his girlfriend in the bath several times and left the knife sticking out. I saw the photos and I've never got the image out of my head. Can't bear to see a knife sticking out of anything. Bread, butter, meat – a pub carvery is the worst. It's OK, Len, it gets to us all some-how.'

I scowl at him, cross that he has passed me the image too, second-hand. We facilitators try not to do this. Our brains are full enough. Poor old Len. I wonder if the effects on him will pass over time, and he can bath his children again. I feel I must share an impact. I tell him about the *Coronation Street* music and Len nods his head.

'Aye, I just leave that to the wife, though. Good excuse for me not to watch it!'

Louise is looking a little uncomfortable at the way this conversation is going.

'What about something you are proud of about the group?'

And we *are* proud of what we have achieved. We did it. We *have* got through to some of them. We did our very best to save another Jessie or Jade or Kelly from abuse, sexual violence and death. Yet I have the uneasy feeling that I can never undo, unhear or unsee what I have experienced in this smelly old group room.

CHAPTER FOURTEEN

PSYCHOPATH

I've noticed over the years that when I meet new people and tell them what I do for a living they always want to hear about the infamous cases. The serial killers. The psychopaths. And the 'worst thing' I have ever heard. I've never told a soul the worst thing I have ever heard and never will. I am afraid of contaminating people. I think about it occasionally when it's triggered, but most of the time it is safely under lock and key.

I train in assessing psychopathy after my first SOTP group finishes. Facilitators have an enforced lie-down period for a couple of months between groups. In this time, I do SOTP assessments and write reports on 'straight' murder cases as a break.

The concept of psychopathy has been around for many years – a theory that some individuals who lurk among us have no conscience, display no remorse, are callous to the core and that this collection of personality traits allows them to commit the most atrocious acts. Dr

Robert Hare, a psychologist and researcher, developed the tool known as the Psychopathy Check List-Revised (PCL-R) to measure this concept.

Dr Hare himself presents the PCL-R training at an anonymous city-centre hotel and Bronwyn and I go along, slightly starstruck. He is something of a celebrity in the world of forensic psychology and certainly the most famous person I have ever met, unless you count dancing with Shaggy at my freshers' ball, or Charlie Bronson. A shrewd white-haired American somewhat lacking in humility, Dr Hare takes us through the twenty traits he believes to represent psychopathy, describing their basis. His fascinating research found four distinct clusters of personality traits/behaviours, namely the domains of interpersonal, affective, lifestyle and antiso-cial. We watch videos of real interviews with psychopathic prisoners and then score their traits on his checklist. To pass the training we must show that we have good inter-rater reliability; that is, we score our practice cases within a reasonable range of the 'gold standard' – the scores that Dr Hare attributed to the case when he assessed it.

I think a lot about Kyle throughout the training. His criminal versatility – many different types of offending; his callousness, not only in his index and previous offending, but evidenced through the cruelty to his dog; his sexual promiscuity, impulsivity and irresponsibility – having two children by the age of eighteen and having never met either; his lack of remorse and empathy. How his characteristics fit so closely with what Dr Hare is explaining. No wonder we struggled with him in the group.

Back at the jail we have a long list of assessments to get through and I am allocated my first PCL-R. Mr Slade has been convicted of the murder of two young women. He is also convicted of attempted kidnap – a 'near miss', where the female victim managed to escape. The offences occurred over a period of five years. According to his detailed police interviews his modus operandi was similar in each case. He would go out driving – or 'hunting', as he described it to the police – and having spotted a lone female walking his way, he would pretend to be broken down in a layby at the side of a quiet road on the way out of a town or village. The boot and bonnet of the car would be open, and he would ask for the victim's help – would she sit in the car and press the accelerator while he fixed the engine, please?

Once the victim was in the car, he would then overpower her, bundle her into the boot, blindfold her and bind her hands and feet with cable ties. In both the murder cases he drove the victims to a nearby wood where he raped and strangled them before hiding them deep in undergrowth. 'But easy enough for the local wildlife to find,' he had told the investigating officers when they found the human remains, partly destroyed by wild animals.

The second victim had smashed the rear-view mirror in her struggle to escape. Mr Slade drove to a garage and got it fixed with the victim still in the boot. The final victim managed to escape by kneeing him in the genitals and flagging down a passing motorist who took her to the police station. She had seen his face, and so followed an extensive manhunt, during which Mr Slade went on the run and drove across Ireland before being captured.

Mr Slade is a 'not to be seen by a lone female' case, so I have a male officer sitting in with me for safety. All interviews are to be recorded for training purposes, so there is an indiscreet 1990s video camera squatting on a cumbersome tripod in the corner of the group work room. It resembles a scene from *The War of the Worlds*. Mr Slade slithers into the room. He has a strong film-star chin, a dramatic Poirot-style full black moustache, groomed shoulder-length hair and long limbs like an octopus.

'Delightful to meet you, Miss Myers,' he croons, extending his slim, bony hand. 'What a lovely way to be spending my morning. Do you mind if I call you Rebecca? Or maybe even Becky? What do you prefer?'

'No shaking hands, Slade,' says the prison officer, saving me.

Mr Slade takes his time in moving the chair we have placed in front of the camera to his own preferred spot and sitting down on it, dramatically crossing his long legs in a quick pincer movement.

'Sorry, Mr Slade, we need to record all these interviews. Would you mind moving the chair back, please?' I say.

'Oh, I am going to be a video star. Wonderful!'

He positions the chair in front of the camera, sits down and smooths his greasy hair like we are about to go live on national TV. I explain the purpose of the interview and why the officer is there. He gives me a little smirk and a prolonged wink, leaning in conspiratorially.

'Yes. That's because they say I'm so dangerous, but I am just a little pussy cat, really. Aren't I, Phil?' He turns to the officer, who ignores him.

'Righty ho, then, Rebecca, shall we start? Do we need Phil to press go, or are we already recording?'

'We are already on, Mr Slade.'

He twirls back to face the camera and flashes it a grin.

We start the assessment, and he runs with it like a kid with a kite. It is hard to keep him on track – he has so many theatrical stories that he wants to tell me. They all seem to portray him as a hero, and he is keen to give me the lengthy and melodramatic details.

'Have you heard that I have a special interest in psychology, Rebecca? Have you read Freud? The Oedipus complex?'

'Not for a while, Mr Slade.'

'I can explain it to you if you like. I sometimes act as a consultant psychologist on the wing, you know, due to my knowledge and experience. The other residents come to me with their problems.'

Out of the corner of my eye I can see Officer Phil sitting behind Mr Slade and rolling his eyes. I cannot look at him in case we make eye contact. I am afraid I might giggle.

We carry on, with me trying to keep Mr Slade on point and failing. I feel like he is the talk-show host and I am the guest, although I figure that in letting him talk, I will be collecting a lot of information on his traits for my checklist.

'Have you ever been cruel to animals?'

'Well, no, not really, Rebecca, unless you count dissection?'

'Tell me a bit more about that, Mr Slade,' I say, although my stomach feels queasy. He scrutinises the camera and strokes his hair again.

'My pleasure. As you know, I have an extraordinary analytical and scientific brain and my science teachers could not keep up with me, so I did my own experiments. Just operating on frogs, snails, you know – small creatures like that, really. No harm done. Even Einstein had to break a few eggs, you know, Rebecca.' He spends some time educating me on the anatomy of a frog. I move him on.

'What sort of jobs have you had, Mr Slade?'

'Well, all sorts of things, really, it just depended on where my varied interests took me. I can turn my hand to most things.'

I have read the file: arson, fraud, deception, assaulting the police, burglary, breaching bail, escape from lawful custody, intimidating/bribing witnesses, handling stolen goods, supplying drugs, theft. Rape, attempted kidnap and two counts of murder. He is correct. He has turned his hand to most things.

'I think my favourite, though … must be working in the abattoir,' he announces.

'Oh, OK, why is that your favourite?'

'Well, I am so good with animals and knowledgeable about their anatomy, my career sort of led me there. I was the abattoir's greatest asset. I used to slaughter the pigs.'

He deadlocks his black eyeballs with mine.

'I would slit the pigs' throats and then stand underneath and drink the warm blood. What do you think of that, Rebecca? How does that fit in with Freud?'

My mouth and throat are as dry as baked sand. He gives me another one of his mocking smiles. I know he is watching for my reaction. I try to swallow and buy myself some time by writing it all down. Play to their sense of enhanced status, I remember Dr Hare saying on the training. A psychopath loves telling you how important they are.

'Er … I am not quite sure.'

'Well, I can probably explain if you would like me to. I know you are only a trainee, after all,' he says, pointing to my prison name badge.

I cannot bear the thought of him explaining how drinking pigs' blood fits with the Oedipus complex. Or how long it will take, given his garrulous tendencies.

'Well, thank you, but we will move on if we can – just aware of the time, Mr Slade.'

'Whatever you say. Now, where are you on your form? Oh, you still have an awful lot to get through – you will get quicker and better at this, I am sure. Come on, let's move on then.'

We are onto the relationships section next. He describes his sexual promiscuity, elaborating on having sex with men, women, prostitutes, and with animals on the farm he grew up on.

'Anything that moves, really, Rebecca. I have the biggest sex drive of anyone I have ever met. And the biggest penis,' he says with sincerity, insisting on extended eye contact and not blinking before I do. His eyes are like granite. They say that the eyes are the windows to the soul, but not in Mr Slade's case. It is like there is no living, breathing thing in there. I break eye contact and he wins.

He seems pleased to be moving onto the section about offending and I ask him why he thought he committed the offences.

'Oh, Rebecca, I've thought about this long and hard, and examined my psychological make-up thoroughly. It's a skill you will be learning as part of your new job, no doubt. Form-u-la-tion, they call it. I'm sure you have studied my file. I am a product of rape, you know. My mother was a single mother and in and out of psychiatric care. I used to go and stay on a farm with a foster family for months at a time and then she would claim me for a bit and neglect me a lot, which was pretty miserable, although I got used to it in the end. I don't think I had the best start, really. But worse things happen at sea. I got involved in some petty crime here and there, as you will have seen on my record. The first time I did it – killed a woman, I mean – I just had this urge to kill a human with my bare hands, and I had to satisfy it. I'd been thinking about it for some time.' He looks at his bony hands, turning them over, like the answers lay in his pale, veiny palms.

'I'd been having deviant masturbatory fantasies. I'm happy to talk you through them if you like.' He is almost purring now.

'Er … I don't think we need to for this assessment … thank you.'

'Oh, that's a shame, I'd like you to hear them.'

It is like he is playing with me for his amusement. Like a cat with a doomed mouse. Somehow, I move him on again. He talks me through what happened with the first victim in detail, even though I have not asked for it. The meticulous preparation he went through and exactly what he did to her. I feel like the temperature in the room has dropped by a degree or two.

'And it satisfied me for a while. The court psychiatrist described it as my "cooling-off period". It's about the only thing he got right. I knew I would do it again. It was like a fire inside and I needed to throw some petrol on it, feed it, you know? I don't like clichés, young Becky, I'm better than that, but it was like a monster inside. I wanted to kill again. I had to.'

He pauses for dramatic effect and studies me closely, his eyes stroking me. I try not to shudder.

'Oh, now then, where *did* you get that pen, Rebecca? Pool Hill Garage? I know that area – lovely, isn't it? Is that where you reside with your … lover?' He treats me to another long wink.

I can feel the hairs on the back of my neck prickling and goosebumps the size of eyeballs growing on my scalp. I'd got the pen free with Polly's last MOT. Now he knows where I live. What a stupid error. I must think quickly. I fake surprise and look at the pen.

'Oh, this? I don't know where I get it from … I er … just borrowed it off the wing, I think …'

'Really, Rebecca! You don't fool me. Next you will be telling me that we are not here to talk about you and can we move on. I know that old psychologist's trick.'

I smile at him. 'Well, you are right, can we move on? I'm really interested in what you have to say.'

He grins again, enjoying our game.

'Flattery will get you everywhere. Now where was I? Oh, yes, my second girl. I got better at it the second time. Got myself a picnic basket in the boot and a picnic rug. No serial killer has a picnic basket, do they? And I was right, it fooled her. I even sat and had a cup of tea out of my Thermos while I was waiting for her. Shame I forgot the sugar. I've always regretted that, although most people say I am sweet enough. The picnic rug came in handy, of course, to roll her in while I got the rear-view fixed. Now that was an exciting moment! But I was too clever, and they were too stupid. I knew they wouldn't look in the boot.'

There is no stopping Mr Slade now. His tap is on full, and I let him flow.

'That one kept me going for a while, but I knew there would be a third – oh, and that last one, she was a clever little minx. But the thrill of the chase, getting the ferry and then driving all over Ireland, Rebecca. I did not think they would catch me. It was like being in a James Bond film! But, of course, they did in the end – fair play to them. I gave them a run for their money, though. It's unfortunate, really, when I look back on it.'

'What's unfortunate? I am not sure I am following you there, Mr Slade.'

'Well, unfortunate that the last one got away. The FBI says you have to top three to be a serial killer. I fell a little short.'

I am exhausted when we reach the end of the interview.

'Thank you, Rebecca, I really enjoyed that. Hope you've learnt a thing or two.'

Mr Slade beams at the camera and gives it a little wave. I almost expect him to take a bow. I switch off the camera, and he reclines in the chair. Legs spread, groin on display. He lights a cigarette, exhaling perfect rings like he is deliciously post-coital.

'Right, Rebecca, now that's off do you want me to tell you a bit more about the animals? I didn't want to say it all on camera in case it made me look bad.'

'Er … if you like Mr Slade,' I say, wishing I had left the camera on as he exposes another level. He reminds me of a poisonous snake I once saw at a tropical centre as a child, shedding its scaly skin.

'Well, there are probably a few more types of animals that I operated on. The fluffy kind, you know. People go mad over fluffy animals, don't they? What is it with puppies and kittens? I don't get it. My foster parents always used to wonder where all the farm kittens went.' He taps the side of his nose with a horny fingernail as if we are sharing an official secret.

'Bye 'eck, lass, you had a live one there, didn't you?' says Officer Phil once Mr Slade's Cat-A book has been signed, he has unravelled his tentacles and loped off to join line route.

'I know, and next time I need to keep the camera on until the end.'

'Aye, he's got more layers than an onion, that one. You did real good with him, though, lass. Held your own.'

Mr Slade is a tough first case and he turns out to be the highest-scoring psychopath we have at Graymoor at the time, gaining almost full marks on the PCL-R. His score is so elevated and he is so intriguing that the video of our interview is used as a practice case on the training of new psychologists across the country. I am mortified when I find out. There are so many things he said that I should have challenged – like 'young Becky' and 'my girl' – and he definitely controlled the interview. Despite Phil's well-meant words, I do not believe I held my own with him. He played with me, and I was out of my depth. I was glad that the camera was focused on his face and not mine when he told me about slurping the pigs' blood.

CHAPTER FIFTEEN

THE EXTENDED PROGRAMME

A few months later, after a few more PCL-Rs and another two weeks spent in a cheap training hotel learning the ropes, Kenny and I sit either side of a familiar blank flip chart ready to facilitate the Extended SOTP Programme. This is another cognitive-behavioural group work programme and the partner of the Core SOTP. It is for high and very high-risk sexual offenders, and Graymoor is packed to its red-slated roof with them.

This time we are in a flimsy, cold Portakabin extending off the department. Programmes are now expanding thick and fast across all jails in the land. A suite of rooms has been quickly added and we have up to five groups running at any one time. I look around the small, low-ceilinged room at my new group. We are much more cramped in here, closer to the men. I am squashed in next to the flip chart. The cheap fluorescent strip lights give out a constant low hum and everyone's face has a disconcerting blue tinge. The smell of fresh paint is almost overbearing, but for now it disguises the smell of the men. Most of the six faces are familiar: Frank, Wayne, Nigel and Jeremy are there. Andy and Kyle are deemed 'not suitably motivated' and will not be joining us for this second period of demanding group treatment. There are two new men.

Sid, aged sixty-three, is convicted of four counts of buggery, six of indecent assault and four of GBH. His offences were against two brothers, aged nine and ten. The victims were the children of his neighbour, and the offences were committed over a period of a few months while he was babysitting them. The GBH offences involved the use of a cane on the victims. Sid has a long list of pre-convictions for sexual assaults against young boys. They date back over forty years. He has been in and out of prison and has finally been given life for the most recent offences.

Sid has been to HM Prison Albany on the Isle of Wight, a specialist sex-offender treatment centre, housing only sex offenders and vulnerable prisoners, and has done the Core SOTP prior to being transferred to Graymoor to complete the Extended SOTP.

Sid has lived a quiet prison life, although he had a couple of warnings at Albany for being in other prisoners' cells and not being where he should be at lock-up. He is now a Listener – a specially selected/trained and trusted prisoner who is available to listen to and support other prisoners who are struggling to cope. He was attacked on remand, stabbed in the neck by a group of prisoners with a shank made from a sharpened toilet brush when he had been outed for his offence. The file states that he was lucky to survive. A previous reader has pencilled in two exclamation marks after this statement.

The second new man, Colin, is serving a life sentence for six counts of indecent assault and eight counts of rape of his stepdaughter. He started abusing her when she was eight years old, and she reported him to her mum when she was sixteen years old. The charges were specimen charges – that is, they are a sample of offences that he committed over the eight years. In long-term child abuse cases, charging for each separate offence is often too difficult given the time passed/number of offences committed and the age of the victim at the time. Colin was thirty at the time of sentence. Now thirty-five, he has no pre-convictions. He lived a previously respectable life as a secondary school teacher, had been the treasurer of the local snooker hall and an active member of the local amateur dramatics society. Colin has no adjudications on his prison file and works in the prison library alongside Jeremy. He is also part of a scheme that helps other prisoners to read.

The four men that I know, despite their previous differences, are huddled together for safety like baby birds in a nest. One of the new men has olive skin, deep-set, sunken eyes, a neatly trimmed beard and a cap of thinning brown hair the colour of a conker. He sits there, tapping his foot, in a clean, tucked-in shirt with a piece of white string for a belt. I am not sure he is allowed the string, although my first impressions are that he isn't the type to break the rules. We have asked the prisoners to introduce themselves and it is his turn next.

'Hello, everyone, I'm Colin. I abused my stepdaughter for eight years. I am a very wicked man.' He looks straight ahead, features taut like he is a sculptor's model.

We turn to the final person in the room, the only one yet to speak. He is a very strange-looking individual. He has grey curtains of chin-length hair, an unkempt handlebar moustache and piercing blue eyes, the colour of the Aegean Sea. I can see a twisted ugly brown scar on his neck, just above his buttoned-up shirt collar, no doubt the result of the shanking. Most noticeable are his huge ears, which are protruding at ninety degrees out of his head. Roald Dahl's BFG could have been modelled on him. I have never seen ears like it, even though he has clearly grown his hair to try to hide them. Additionally, he appears to have somewhat enlarged breasts. I try not to stare as I know exactly how it feels to be on the receiving end of prolonged chest-level interest. Frank doesn't have the same social controls and is gazing open-mouthed as the interloper speaks.

'Hello, all, I'm Sid,' he says in a gentle, measured tone, as if he is leading a yoga class. 'Good to be back in treatment. I've come from Albany.'

'Can you tell us your offences, please, Sid?' says Kenny. 'Just a brief description. We like to get it all out in the room.'

'Of course, pal,' says Sid. 'I'm used to this. I've offended against young boys, on and off for forty years. The off bits are when I was in prison. I finally got life for indecently assaulting two boys a few years ago, before Albany and my treatment. I have changed my life now.'

I cannot help but notice his immediate minimisation of his convictions, which I know include buggery and violence to the victims. We do not press him. There will be plenty of time for that. I remember Elizabeth's wise words that this is a man telling a group of strangers about his most embarrassing secret.

Over the session the six men give a brief active account of their offending. All have done SOTP, so we do not have the CDs to unpick, but there are some that have sneaked through the net. I know the accounts of the men from my earlier group, but Sid's and Colin's are new.

Sid's active account goes something like this: 'I was bullied as a child, because of my ears, and developed very low self-esteem. A man abused me and so I just went on to abuse others myself. Thanks to Albany I have accepted that I am homosexual, and I would now like to have relationships with younger men, but not boys as I know it's illegal.'

'*Just* went on to abuse others,' says Jeremy. 'Isn't that a CD, Sid? I thought you have been to Albany. You should know better. I did the SOTP with Rebecca here,' he waves his hand towards me like he is swatting away a fly, 'and *even I* know not to say things like that.'

'Thank you so much for picking that up, Jeremy,' says an unrattled Sid. 'One of the things Albany taught me is to be open to feedback. You are right, it is a CD. I was abused and then I went on to do it myself. That's an explanation, not an excuse, though, right?'

He cocks his head to one side as if his enormous ears are helping him hear things we cannot. Like aliens or those funny dog whistles. I am almost laughing at the thought of it and have to compose myself.

'That sounds like you are blaming the abuse now, don't it, Miss?' says Frank, turning to me as usual for confirmation. I am pleased he has been selected for this group.

'What do *you* think, Sid?' I ask, relying on an age-old facilitator favourite.

'I am grateful for the feedback,' he says with the composure of a neurosurgeon. 'I analysed my own abuse at Albany. We got the opportunity to do that there; they specialise in men like me. My abuse is not an excuse, or a CD; it's an explanation, like I said. I did not do it because I was abused, but on the other hand, if I hadn't been, I may not have done it. My abuse changed me as a person, and I think you can't ignore it.'

He has clearly picked up some therapy bites at Albany that work for him; however, I also agree with him. How can you ignore it? Child abuse does impact the way children view the world. We will be delving far deeper in this group. I am worried about Wayne and what secrets his childhood hold.

'I think there is a difference between an excuse and an explanation,' I say, and I explain that on this programme we are going to be considering how and where their offending comes from. Examining their childhoods, early development and relationships, and looking for connections. We will be considering the role of sexual fantasy. We will be making links and searching for patterns. Well, hopefully we will, I think to myself. I am aware that this group is more complex and the concepts more abstract than the Core SOTP. Hopefully I will be able to make the insightful psychological links required and prove myself as a 'proper' forensic psychologist.

Jeremy nods in satisfaction. Wayne rubs a scar on his forearm. He is back to wearing short-sleeved T-shirts. I notice it and cast a glance at Kenny. He has seen it too.

'Don't worry, we are not going to be asking for any specific details about childhood, unless you want to talk about it,' he says to everyone.

Kenny and I have bonded as facilitators already. It is as if an invisible wire stretches across the flip chart and connects us, letting our thoughts slide, bounce and whirl across it. I smile at him in thanks. He is like a loyal dog. One with a permanently wagging tail who just really wants to please. I know that I can trust him. There are only the two of us in the facilitator team, so we will be delivering every session together. Resources are scarce. We have far more sex offenders and groups to run than psychologists and facilitators available, and the pressure is on to try to meet the ever-increasing yearly targets.

'OK, Colin, your turn next then,' I say.

Colin pauses and rubs his thighs with his hairy hands, which I note are devoid of the customary yellow nicotine stains.

'OK, as I said, I abused my stepdaughter. It was very serious abuse, and I am very ashamed. It went on a very long time. I was very violent. I was cruel. I was unhappily married. And the worst thing is, I was a teacher and I should have known better. I pleaded guilty.'

It seems an open account on the face of it, but the men are on him, trained by their experiences of the SOTP to prod and press into any story and potential anomaly they hear.

'While I welcome a fellow professional to the group, Colin, what is the relevance of you being a teacher?' asks Jeremy, back to his cross-examination mode. 'Did you abuse the children in your care too?'

Colin glares at him.

'No, I certainly did not, and I will thank you for not asking me that again. Or insinuating it. I was never charged with any offences other than those against my stepdaughter.'

'What does in-sin-uatin' mean, Miss?' says Wayne, out of his depth.

'It means implying, Wayne,' says Jeremy, peering down his long nose at Colin. 'Well, the relevance is that children will have surrounded you and you clearly have an interest in them, so I was only asking. Just to let you know, Colin, I was a sergeant in the police, so I know a bit about asking questions, as it happens. And simply because you are never charged doesn't mean it never happened. I was in the police, as I said, so I know exactly what happens on arrest and with the CPS – that's the Crown Prosecution Service for the rest of you. Saying all that, I hope we can communicate as two professionals together for the rest of the group.'

Colin stares at him, mouth as thin-lipped as a mussel.

'Er, thanks, Jeremy,' says Kenny. 'Questions are always good, but we are here to focus on the offences that Colin is convicted of. Now let's move on a bit. One of the first jobs in this group for you all is going to be to draw a life map. This is going to help us try to understand how you came to be the person you are today. We want you to look back over your lives and think about the events that have affected how you think and see the world, yourself and others. This is your homework. You will get a whole session each to present back.'

We give out long sheets of blank wallpaper and colourful marker pens and go through what is expected of them. Frank asks lots of questions so he can get it right. Jeremy takes copious notes in a notebook he springs from his top pocket and makes it his job to share out the pens. Sid rolls up the sheet and tucks it under his arm without a word and they all troop out.

'I think that went OK,' says Kenny as we sit down for our debrief in the group room.

'Yeah,' I say. 'I'm a bit worried about Wayne, though. He is picking his scabs and I am sure he was abused as a child. It's going to be tough for him.'

'It will. But we can watch out for him. How are things with Daniel?'

'Intense,' I say as Daniel appears at the door.

'Now then, you two,' he says with a smile. He selects a chair next to me and puts his hand on my knee. 'Just thought I would check on you both. You're taking ages. I was waiting for you in the smoke room and wondered what you were getting up to.'

'No worries, mate,' says Kenny with one of his big, relaxed smiles. 'She's all yours now, we are done. See you in the morning, Becky.' He gives me a wink as he closes the door.

'What's with the *Becky*?' asks Daniel. 'And why don't you plan and debrief in your office like we used to do on our group? Seems silly, you being all the way up here and alone together.'

'It's fine, we like doing it up here. Kenny and I are just really good mates. Why? Are you jealous?'

Daniel laughs but his eyes do not crease.

'No,' he says, leaning forward, squeezing my knee. 'But I am watching ... work in your office instead from now on, yeah?'

CHAPTER SIXTEEN

LIFE MAPS

The next morning Kenny and I sit in my office, prepping for the group. I am painting my nails as usual before I go on show. I hate having chipped nails. Polished on the outside equals feeling prepared on the inside. Daniel and I have come into work together today. He left his wife at the weekend and moved into his own flat. We have been playing happy families, although it hasn't felt that happy. I've noticed his not-so-subtle attempts to influence what I wear. Persistent phone calls to and from his wife, with him checking out her new sex life. As he strutted in from the car park holding my hand, several officers nodded and smiled. I have enhanced my status among them, but I feel like a harlot.

'We ready? We know what we are doing today, don't we? Let's just go with it,' says Kenny.

He is so laid-back about the sessions and seems so confident in his own abilities. I want to borrow a bit of it. I love working with him. I know Daniel is worried I like it a bit too much. We pack our pens and flip chart and head to the group room.

'So, group,' I say when they have all settled in their now-usual chairs and quietened down. 'We are going to start the life maps today. Jeremy, I am sure you are really well prepared, and we would like you to go first. Let's have a look at your map – spread it out on the floor between us and everyone can gather round.'

Jeremy straightens up with pride at my praise of his organisational skills and starts to unroll his wallpaper onto the carpet tiles. There isn't much room as everyone leans in. The map is orderly and colour coordinated. His handwriting is in tiny, elegant capital letters and appears as if it has been transcribed using a ruler and a calligraphy pen.

'I have prepared this just as was asked. Here is the key on the side showing the corresponding colours for major life events, thoughts, feelings and behaviour, so you can all follow as I am presenting. And I know we are drawing out unhelpful patterns of thinking as we go, so I have made a little start. Hope that is not jumping the gun.' He beams and the patch of disobedient hair at his fringe waggles around merrily.

'Less said about you and guns, the better, I would imagine,' says Colin with a snort.

Frank and Wayne exchange a glance and there is a discreet smile at Frank's mouth.

'Well, Colin, I don't know what group you were on before, but we value respect here, and we never criticise each other's offences,' says Jeremy.

''Part from when you used to go on at me 'n' Kyle 'bout our burglaries and call us common criminals,' says Wayne.

'I think Jeremy has the key word here; it's about respect, and we do really value that in all the groups we run. If we can all be mindful of that, please, let's continue. Jeremy, it looks like you have done a really detailed job of this life map, well done. Let's hear it. Group, remember that as we are going through, we will be helping Jeremy to see any patterns of thinking that appear in his life,' I say.

Jeremy slides Colin a final hard stare, grants me a microscopic dip of his head and turns to his work.

This is Jeremy's story:

I was born to a hard-working non-criminal family and have one older step-brother who had already left home for medical school. He was a lot older than me, and my parents were already old when I was born – my dad was sixty. I had my tonsils out when I was five and was told not to cry, so I did not. I excelled at school but never had a girlfriend when I was young like my friends did, although I did fancy a couple of girls. They never seemed to fancy me back. I was a bit scared of them really and did not know what to say. I preferred my studies and showing my parents I could do well. Eventually one girl agreed to go out with me, and we went to the cinema. I was about sixteen. I really liked her and told her I really fancied her and had done for a long time. She opened my jeans and touched my penis during the film, and I ejaculated very quickly on her hand. She jumped up and told everyone in the seats around us. I was mortified.

'What were you thinking at the time, Jeremy?' I ask.

'Like I've put here on the map, I can't believe it. Why has she done that? She didn't need to tell everybody! Why?'

'What did you think of her?'

'I thought she had let me down. I told her that I really liked her, and then she did that to me.'

'What did this teach you?' It is like mining for his thoughts and beliefs.

'Not to show my emotions or tell anyone how I am feeling.'

'Do you see this type of thinking anywhere else in your life?' asks Kenny, now trying to explore if this is a more general pattern of thinking.

'Very much. I was always told not to cry by my father – "real men don't cry". It's best face and foot forward. Shall I carry on?' We give him the go-ahead.

After that incident I put girls out of my mind and concentrated on school and college and sport. I was captain of our local youth cricket team and won best player. I just wanted to be the best and prove myself. I applied to the police force and went to training college at Hendon. I passed out as the top recruit that intake. I loved the order, the rules and the uniform. The respect. 'The Job', as we called it. I felt superior to members of the public. I apprehended a burglar with a knife. He had taken a woman hostage in her house, and I got a Commendation. I was so proud. I attended a suicide where someone shot himself. It was very messy, bits of brain everywhere, but I held it together, all my emotions. I had learnt that they are a sign of weakness, but it was a strength in The Job. My colleagues who attended with me fell apart. I knew I needed to stay in control … There you go, that's the control again …

I still had no girlfriend and was a virgin. My brother tried to get me to go with a prostitute, but I did not want to. I want a woman to want me and for it not to be dirty and sordid. Besides, I was a serving police officer – it was beneath me. I got promoted to sergeant. I needed to show I was the best, make my parents proud. But there was no show of pride from them when I told them. I joined a local shooting club for a hobby. I was a very good shot and hoped one day to join the firearms section of the police. I had a gun I kept at home – all legal, of course. The other coppers all teased me about not having a girlfriend, but I just wanted to focus on my career. I did think about it a lot, though, and saw a TV programme about a man who was a fifty-year-old virgin. I was worried that would be me.

I bought my own house on a nice street. Everything was perfect apart from the fact that I did not have a girlfriend. I started to think about sex a lot and about getting a girlfriend. I liked one of the WPCs at work and asked her out, but she turned me down and then told everyone. I was so humiliated. Here we go again; women are determined to show me up. They cannot be trusted. I won't let myself down again like this. Showing I liked her was stupid. I need to keep my emotions in check.

'Why was this so important?' I ask.

'So I would not get hurt. So I stayed in control.'

'Why did you need to be in control?'

'So I don't get hurt, like I said. It keeps a lid on it. My lid. Emotion is a sign of weakness.' He carries on with his story:

Moving on: an attractive divorced woman with two kids moved in next door. She was older than me. She will know about sex – maybe she can teach me, maybe she will be grateful for a relationship. We started talking over the fence, saying hello. I will never tell her I like her or ask her out, but I want her to teach me about sex. Perhaps I can persuade her. If I can persuade her, then maybe she will end up liking me and be my girlfriend. It's a ready-made family. What will my parents think? They will be proud, like they are of my brother – the doctor – and his family. I started thinking about how to persuade her. Will she be willing? Maybe she won't. Maybe if I take my gun, she will be persuaded. I read a book where a man did that, and the woman liked it.

'What do you mean by "persuaded", Jeremy?' says Kenny.

'Well … encourage her. It's what I thought at the time, like you asked for.'

'What do you think now?'

'As you know from the Core SOTP, it is rape, isn't it? I was planning rape.' He continues.

I thought about it for at least six months, what it would be like, where it would happen. I did not want it to be at her house in case her kids came home, or her ex-husband popped in. I started to think about a picnic, being outdoors. I always liked the idea of outdoor sex. I can lay a blanket down and we can make love. There was a field with long grass and a wood at the end of the road.

'Isn't "makin' love" tho'. It's rape, Jeremy. Just say it, man,' says Wayne.

'Yes, it is, but I did not see it at the time. I thought you wanted my thoughts at the time. I'm only sticking to the rules here, for Christ's sake.'

'We do want your thoughts. I think the group are finding it difficult to hear you saying these words to describe a rape,' I say, distracted by the description of the picnic rug. *What is it with offenders and picnic rugs?* I drag my thoughts away from the unforgettable Mr Slade and back to the group.

'Well, I would have had sexual intercourse with her, whatever, with her consent or not. Happy now? I'll carry on if I am allowed,' he says with the snarling lip of an irate terrier.

Anyhow, I was planning it for some time, and I picked a nice summer's day when I knew I had a shift off, and the children were at school. I was very nervous and excited. I took the gun and some rope – yes, to tie her or gag her if she refused. It was happening. I knocked on her door and she answered in a very skimpy vest top, inviting me into the hallway. She had no bra on.

Jeremy pauses. 'I have highlighted my CDs here, so you don't all have a go at me,' he says, casting a defensive glance around the room.

Well, that's it, it's happening. She likes me (CD). She has got that top on for me (CD). It's now or never. I will do this. I asked her to come for a walk and a picnic. I had my shooting clothes on, my gun and a picnic basket of food. She said she has things to do and can't come. I thought, there's no way you are turning me down. I am not going through this again. You women and your mixed messages. For once, I am getting what I want here.

I showed her the gun underneath my coat and told her to come with me, we were going for a walk. She came with me. See? It's going well. She likes me (CD). We will just have sex and I will bring her home unharmed (CD). I will no longer be a virgin. We walked down the street and into the field and long grass. I was so aroused, but I was worried about premature ejaculation, like in the cinema. I put the blanket down and the food. It was a lovely picnic. It is going to be OK, no harm done (CD). I told her to lie down. She was very calm and started talking to me about what I was doing. She is not afraid (CD). I gagged her with the rope and tied her hands. I laid the gun next to us. I began to rape her, tenderly (CD).

There was a man with a dog. Fuck, what is happening? This cannot happen. I am not letting anyone spoil this. It is my moment. I am the one call-ing the shots here, not you. I need to get things back on track, do things my way. It's me in charge. I am in

control of this. I picked up the gun and shot him and
the dog. They both died at the scene.

I allow a moment's silence. The room needs it. I ask
Jeremy what patterns he can see across his life map.

'Well, they are about not showing my emotions and
liking to be in charge,' Jeremy says. 'It's obvious now. I
can see it.'

'And something 'bout women?' says Wayne. 'Know I
have got some problems about women too, just not
worked it out yet.'

'Yes, thank you, Wayne,' says Jeremy. 'I was coming to
that. I don't think that they can be trusted at all. They
never actually say what they really mean.'

He isn't looking at me, but given that I am the only
woman in the group it feels rather awkward.

'Have you ever trusted any woman, Jeremy?' Kenny
asks.

'No, never, and look at how I have ended up because
of it. What a waste of my life and my career. And the
victims', of course,' he adds hastily.

Jeremy talks for the whole session. He does not like
being interrupted for questions; he wants to stick to the
map and explain every event he has written about in
irrelevant detail. It is tricky to get the group to focus on
the thoughts: they keep hearing the situations and wanting to know more. We must guide them and model the

sort of questions we want them to ask. 'What were you thinking when that happened? Can you see any links between what you thought then, and other times in your life?'

I am shattered after the session. Exploring the life map is like wading through treacle. I open a window as far as I can; the air in the tiny room is so thick with sweat and tobacco smoke I can feel it resting on me, like a surplus epidermis. The scent of fresh paint has evaporated.

'Want to debrief in your office today?' asks a knowing Kenny.

'No,' I say. 'We are fine up here.'

I am aware that this will irritate and annoy the jealous Daniel. He has been phoning, visiting and talking about his ex-wife far too much. Whenever she calls, he goes running back. As Princess Diana put it so well: it is like there are three of us in the relationship. I think he deserves a bit of his own medicine. I am in revenge mode. Sure enough, within minutes Daniel appears at the door.

'Coming down, *Becky*?' he says.

'Soon. Kenny and I are discussing the session and with confidentiality and all that, we need to be alone, sorry.'

Daniel glares at me and turns his back. I know he will punish me in some way for it later, but I have had enough of him and his pathetic battles and jealousy. *It works both ways, Daniel. I'm in control today.* Hang on … haven't we just been identifying that pattern in Jeremy? Am I any different?

'You sure you're OK?' Kenny asks when we hear Daniel's firm footsteps reach the end of the makeshift corridor and his keys turning in the gate.

Kenny can see right through me. I relay the recurring tearful rows, the ugly jealousy and the crowded relationship. How there has even been a threat of suicide from Daniel. How I have to tiptoe around his feelings like Father Christmas on Christmas Eve, never knowing what will stir, shift or break if I put a foot wrong.

'What an earth are you doing with him then, Bec?'

I have no reasonable answer.

'What's worse though, Kenny, is that I think I might have the same thinking pattern as Jeremy.'

'Well, why don't we do our own life maps? Look at our own thinking? It might be fun?'

I am not sure about fun. But if I can go there, to some of the painful stuff in my boxes, I think it might help me be a better psychologist.

CHAPTER SEVENTEEN

DELVING DEEPER

Over the next few weeks the group rolls on, gathering a momentum of its own, and the rest of the men work through their life maps.

Sid goes next.

I was born, and that same day my dad left. I wasn't wanted from the start. I knew this straight away. It did not take Albany to work that out. My much older sister got pregnant and left when I was six, so it was just my mum and me. She only had one leg and would get very down and depressed and stay in bed. I had to care for her. I had to wash her all over, including her vagina. It was ugly and it frightened me. I never wanted to do it, but I had no choice. I am very strange-looking, as you can see. A social misfit, with a one-legged mother. As you can imagine, I was bullied from the off. Nobody at school liked me, the girls laughed at my ears and I knew there was never any chance as long as I lived that I would ever get to have sex with one. And I did not want to. Girls and vaginas frightened me. I am a freak.

He adds: 'Can you see the pattern here. Is it clear?' We all nod back.

'As crystal,' says Colin.

I tried to keep my mum at home, like she was a secret. As well as having one leg, she was a loony. Best kept out of the way. I had one friend at school called Bobby. Like me, he was a misfit. He had a back brace and leg braces. It was like he lived in a cage. He always had problems breathing too. At school one day he showed me his willy under the desk. It was very exciting, and I showed him mine. We were caught and taken to be caned by the headmaster. He asked to see both of our willies, so we got them out, and then he caned us again. I learnt two or more things (Albany again). We have not been careful enough. Sex is to be kept hidden and a secret. Willies are exciting. Other men like willies too. At Albany I learnt that I associated sex and pleasure with pain at this point. I was about twelve. At Albany they called them the 'formative years' and it is a very important stage for sexual development. I've been through all this before as you can see. The headmaster called me in a few times a week after that and abused me. Sometimes Bobby was there too. It was our secret. I got used to the abuse. I was a bit frightened at first, that he would hurt us, but in the end I got used to it and I liked sharing what was happening with Bobby. I would get an erection, which confused me, but the headmaster told me that was normal and a sign that I liked it and was growing up normally. He used the cane a lot. I liked the attention, I suppose.

Bobby and I touched each other sometimes – in fact, quite a lot. I enjoyed it and it felt different with him. It was the only part of my life that I liked. He did not see me as a freak – well, maybe he did but he was one himself, so it did not matter. One day I went to school and Bobby was not there. He had died from his illness. No one told me. This is when I developed my 'fuck everyone' attitude. He was my only friend; why did no one tell me? Why did that happen to me? Fuck them all. I hate everyone. No one will want me now. And I was right, no one did. I was fifteen.

The headmaster retired and the only humans that would talk to me were younger boys, aged about ten or eleven. I had a paper round so I would spend my wages on stuff they wanted: sweets, drinks and crisps. One day I took a couple of them into the fields and gave them a cigarette in exchange for a peep and a touch. It was here that I learnt to groom. I hope everyone knows that word. It's from Albany. I told myself there is no harm done; they like it. Just like I do. It's only what happened to me.

This carried on until I was caught and put into Borstal. I hated it. I hated the screws. I hated everyone. The only thing good about it was the other boys. There was lots of experimental sex – it's what happens when you put lots of boys or men together. They have sex.

Sid then says, 'You all know yourselves from being in prison that men can "turn" when serving life, and "turn back" on release. I know you all know.'

You could have heard a feather float into the room, and there is an objection from Frank and Jeremy.

'Speak for yourself, Sid.'

Sid gives one of his knowing smiles.

I learnt how to keep it all a secret. I bribed the younger boys if they did not want to do things to me. I was offending inside prison. I had full sex for the first time. There was no going back.

I spent the next thirty years of my life doing the same thing. I worked on and off as a painter and decorator – skills I learnt thanks to Her Majesty. I would befriend single mothers and families with young boys and offer to do the odd job for free to get in their houses. Even specialised in children's bedrooms. I am ashamed to say I planned it all. I think I was born like that, but I can see my experiences shaped me too: my mother and the abuse and Bobby. My abuse did no harm, so I know I will never hurt the boys (yes, I know, CD). It was always very gentle (CD). They always agreed (CD) and I did no harm (CD). It is the way I was born; I can't help it (CD). I can't stop. Boys are beautiful to me, and I cannot give them up (CD). These are all the CDs that I told myself for years.

I went in and out of prison, getting longer and longer sentences, but never being able to stop. I was an expert at secrets. I could have worked for MI6. My looks never improved, as you can see, and it always kept adults and especially women at a distance. For some reason the boys did not mind. I just became an older, uglier freak. On one prison sentence I was given some injections – you know, to help with my sexual urges for boys. I wanted to stop; I really did. It was like a castration, but I didn't have anything chopped off, and before I knew it I was dead below the waist. I didn't mind but then I started to grow breasts and have palpitations, so they had to stop. Maybe the dose was too big. I knew I would offend again anyway.

In my late fifties I abused my neighbour's children. She was a bad mother and I had taken pity on the boys. I used to babysit them when she went out drinking, buy them fish and chips, let them watch films they shouldn't. I started sexually abusing them. One day I bought a cane and used it on the boys. Things got out of hand. I am ashamed to think about it now. I am glad one of them told the teacher. I was caught and given a life sentence. I hated everyone in life at the time – the police, the judge, everyone – but now I see it as the best thing that has ever happened to me. It was the start of my new life. I went to Albany and, as you can see, came out a changed man. I am a homosexual man. I will now only have sex with boys over eighteen. I admit to still having an interest in boys, but I now know it's wrong.

'Thanks to Albany,' mutters Wayne. 'Of course it's fuckin' wrong.'

Sid pretends he hasn't heard. 'Would you like me to summarise my patterns of thinking? I know them off by heart. Fuck everyone in society. I am a freak; no one wants me. Things have got to be kept secret.'

Nigel has been quiet up until now. 'I can see some similarities between me and you, Sid. It has been very helpful. I'm struggling with my map, but I knew I would. I wonder if I can have one of those injections – you know, to help me?'

'That's what treatment is all about,' chirps Sid. 'Learning from one another. Glad to be of help, pal. I'm not sure they do the injections anymore – it was years ago – but they do leave you lifeless below. There's no chance of getting it up once it's taken hold, you know, Nige.'

I know that Sid is talking about anti-androgen injections, which significantly lower testosterone. Essentially a chemical castration, and a voluntary, rather extreme but effective option rarely used in prisons these days, the reversible injections help control sexual urges. I've not met anyone who has had them before, but I know the side-effects can be alarming, hence the noticeable breast tissue Sid has developed.

'Don't need a penis to offend, though, do you, Sid?' says Jeremy bluntly. 'Not while you've still got your hands' – he waves his wildly, as if to demonstrate his point – 'and your brain.'

Jeremy has made the point for me. As is obvious from the sessions we are running, sexual offending is about so much more than sex.

It is tough listening to all the stark details of Sid's abuse of boys. He presents with no embarrassment, like he is chatting about what he has been watching on TV that week. At least Nigel has the decency to be ashamed and self-conscious about what he has done. Child abuse is the pinnacle of wickedness in our society. Yet we must stomach hearing the sickening details in the group for the sole purpose of trying to stop it happening to other children. I reason this is a good enough cause to tolerate it. I have to mould an engaged and interested expression on my face, like it is clay, when I am working with Sid. I notice Wayne distancing himself from Sid in the group room. Jeremy seems to regard him as a conundrum that he needs to crack, asking lots of questions about Sid's childhood and taking notes, which we have to ask him to destroy.

The next session it is Wayne's turn, and he looks like we are about to throw him in with caged wolves. He is very pale and grips his life map to his chest. The other men are gathered round ready, knees almost touching in the confined space. I can see Jeremy making sure Sid's splayed knees do not touch his own.

'Shall we roll that out then, Wayne?' asks Kenny.

'Er, yeah. I'm not that good at reading and writing, so I've done loadsa pictures.'

'Brilliant, suits me,' says Kenny with his warmest smile.

This is Wayne's story:

The first thing I remember is me little sis being born. And I 'ated her from the start cos she took all the attention. S'long as I can remember my stepdad beat my mum and me – worst when he had bin drinking. His dad was the same and was in prison for murdering his wife – he had battered her for years. I 'ated me stepdad and only liked me mum. By the time I was five I was runnin' away from home. To stop me, me stepdad tied me hands together and then tied me to the radiator in their bedroom with the dog lead. Then he went out drinking. My mum dared not untie me. I did not get me tea. Why did she not do anythin'? Why me? When he came home, he beat me mum and then raped her on the bed wi' me watchin'. She was bleedin' from her mouth and nose and I know it will be me next for a beatin'. I was really scared. I thought he was going to kill her, and I wet meself. Me stepdad beat me worse than normal cos he said I had ruined the carpet. He said I was worse than the dog and gave me dog food for me tea from the floor when I was still tied to the radiator. He did not untie me, so I had to eat it like an animal just wi' me mouth from the dog bowl.

A dense curtain of silence sweeps across the room. I know Wayne's life has been traumatic. The self-harm scars give him away. So do his prickly reactions when we talk about the abuse of children by the other group members.

'That sounds like a really difficult time for you, Wayne. What did you think about what was happening to you?' I say, trying to focus on his reaction to the event and how it influenced his life, rather than the event itself. It feels callous to be focusing on the job and asking him these questions. Surely he needs some counselling. I am worried he is too broken for us to mend.

'I was no good. No one loved me. No one cared. Why

me? The next bit is gonna be really difficult for me, but I wanna say it, cos I ain't told no one before.'

It is sleeting outside and the gloom of the dull winter afternoon soaks into the dingy room like we have a leak. I know what is coming next.

'OK, Wayne, tell us what you need to. We are listening and you can trust us.'

'Me mum abused me when I was ten – sexually, I mean. Loads of times. She made me do things to her. Really bad things, like.'

Only the group-room clock speaks. I do not know what to say. I peek at Kenny. Poor Wayne. This is really tough. I want to reach out and put my hand on his shoulder and comfort him. If it was anyone else and not a prisoner, I would. He is just another sad human. Yet I cannot break the boundaries. He is a serial rapist in treatment. I send him a sympathetic smile that he does not see.

'You have been very brave telling us that, Wayne. We don't need to know any more details, unless you want to tell us. How did it make you feel at the time?'

'Angry and confused and ashamed.'

'And what did you think about what your mother did, and about yourself at the time?'

'Why me? Is this what is s'posed to happen when you get to be ten? Nobody loves me. I am a waste of space. I knew it was wrong and I hated my mum for it. But I loved her too. I was really confused. I knew I would get her back one day. I was just waiting. Anyways, I've said it now.' He carries on.

Me stepdad was still using us all as a punchbag and mum was abusin' me. One day I am gonna get you back, you fuckers. I started drinkin' and smokin' weed and hangin' out with the bad kids. They got me stealin' but at least I had someone to hang out with. I watched some porn DVDs with me mates – they was nasty but a bit of me liked it. That's how you punish women. That's shown her, the fuckin' bitch. I thought like that about me mum too, but I loved her, that was me problem. I started having thoughts about havin' sex with her, rough like on the DVDs, and I'd have a wank. Then I'd feel bad 'n' confused. Fucked up. I got taken into care eventually, my behaviour was so bad. No one loved or cared about me.

'You keep saying that, Wayne,' says Frank.

'It's true, mate, no one does. I was no good, one big fuck-up. Still am. Sorry, Miss, for the language.'

'I think that's one of them pattern thingies,' says Frank.

I was still takin' drugs and stealin'. I didn't give a shit anymore. Then some woman at the kids' home, she abused me too. She was s'posed to care. She would come in at night with some weed for me, and then do it. I let her cos at least I got the weed, and I was away from me stepdad. They are all the same (women). One day I will get me own back, get even. After a bit I got caught for all the stealin' and put in a detention centre for three months. I was fourteen by then. No one cared – yes, I know, there I go again, but I was just a waste of space and had no one. There is more porn and drugs in there than I have ever seen. I learnt to handle meself. I was in and out of care and Borstal then, cos I kept doin' burglary and crime every time they let me out. I'd got nowt to lose. When I was eighteen, I met Shaz. She was really nice. I wanted to marry her, and the sex was great. She let me be a bit rough.

'What do you mean, "a bit rough" and she "let" you?' says Sid.

Wayne cannot look at him and says to Kenny, 'You know, a bit of a slap an' that. She liked it. Well, maybe she didn't; maybe it's all CD. I don't know what's real anymore. This group, it's fuckin' me right up.'

'You are doing really well though, Wayne. We know it's difficult. Your behaviour with Shaz, how does it link with your offending, do you think?' says Kenny.

'I dunno.'

'Well, what thoughts did you have about that sort of sex?'

'As I said, I liked it.'

'Why did you like it?'

'It made me feel like more of a man, like I was doing what I wanted. Like I had a bit of power and say so for once. I liked Shaz, though.'

'Those thoughts, Wayne. Are they part of a pattern of thinking?'

'Yeah, s'pose.'

'How do they link with your offending?'

'Well, s'pose it's like what I thought then. I liked being in control and doing what I wanted with my victims.'

'I'm really pleased you can see that. Let's carry on,' says Kenny with a smile.

I kept on wiv the drugs and doing burglaries to order now, and I got caught and put back in prison. Shaz finished with me. I knew she would – fuck women, they are all the same. Fuck everyone. I will get my own back one day. When I came out, I have never bin so angry. I went to see me mum – found out where she lived cos she had split wiv me stepdad and disowned me, not that I cared. Her boyfriend was out. I tied her up with a dog lead and hit her with a broom handle. Then I assaulted her, sexually like, with my fingers. I was rough and she cried. I got my own back and it felt good. But it felt bad too, after – really bad. She told the police. I did not think she would dare, cos of the abuse, but she did. I served another sentence and came out hating her and meself even more.

And my life just went on like that. I had a few girl-friends, but it never lasted. I kept on wiv the drugs, and they got harder: speed, pills, anythin'. I was robbin' to pay for the drugs. I had no one and knew I'd fucked up, that I was a failure. Then I did that burglary, where I saw the woman's underwear, and you know the rest. I wore that gorilla mask. I wanted to scare them. I wanted to feel like an animal. I was getting my own back, every time I did it. I was getting my own back. For once, it was going as I wanted it. Fuck everyone else. I liked the feelin' it gave me, powerful and strong. I liked tyin' them up and takin' the knife. I liked smashin' the lights and cutting their phone wires. I was buzzing. I would feel shit the next day and think I am no better than me mum or me stepdad and want to kill meself. That didn't last and then I would wanna do it again, so I did. I don't think I would 'ave stopped if the pigs – sorry, police – hadn't caught me.

'I don't think you have said that before, Wayne, about how much you enjoyed it at the time, or that you would not have stopped. That's very honest,' I say.

'Now I've done the Core I know the damage I did. I fucked up, but I need to change. And I am bein' honest, as honest as I can, for all me victims' sakes. I've got to stop. I hate meself for what I have done, Miss.'

'And what patterns of thinking can you see across your life map?'

'Well, like I says. I'm no good, am I? One big fuck-up,' he says with a sniffle. 'That's me main one. And that sommat you said before about liking the power wiv me victims. I've got that too.'

'OK, you've done well to spot those two. In your own words, what do you think it is about "power"?'

'It is about wanting to be the boss, for once. All me life I'd not been, what wiv me mum and me stepdad and the care-home woman.'

'And you have something about women too,' says Frank.

'Yeah, well, I thought they was all the same and I wanted to get my own back. 'Specially on me mum.'

'I think that's two patterns, Wayne, not one,' offers Jeremy.

'Yeah, all right then, there's another two. Women are all the same and I've got to get me own back. That's four.'

'Then there's the "no one loves me" stuff,' says Sid. 'That sounds like a victim-type stance to me. We covered a lot about that at Albany.'

'OK, well, that's five then. That's more than anyone else. Why have I got so many? Just shows I'm one big fuck-up and there is sommat wrong wiv me, like I told you.'

I can see that Wayne is using the pattern of thinking right there and then. He is actually in it.

'Well, we all have a few strong patterns; some of us have more than others,' I say. 'But don't worry about that now. We'll be looking at these patterns a bit more when we've done the life maps.'

'Really? You 'ave 'em too, Miss? And you, Kenny? Well, you two ain't done what we've done, have you? There's nowt wrong wiv you.'

After they have all gone back to the wing, Kenny and I sit as usual and talk about the session. I am always conflicted after working with Wayne. There is something so childlike about him – his wide face, broom-bristle eyelashes and primary-age grammar. The ghost of the damaged young boy chained to the radiator lingers. I want to go back in time, untie that broken little boy and take him home for a hot meal and some parental love. I can picture the dirty, violent bedroom and the cold metal radiator. I now know why he reacted so strongly to being tied up in the victim empathy role plays. And then there was the sexual abuse. How can a mother do that to her child?

I can see that his mother is a victim too, but somehow it seems worse that she was the sexual abuser. Society does not cope well with female sexual offenders. They smash the caring female stereotype. Men have heightened testosterone; they are the hunters and have been out killing since the beginning of time. Women care for the cave. Perhaps this reaction was also due to my own childhood experiences. While never abused, I struggle to delete the imprint of being left by my own mother in my formative years. Mothers are not supposed to do that. Mothers are supposed to stick by their children and put them first, come what may. The damage caused by poor mothering creeps down the generations like silent bad blood. My mother blames her mother. I vow that if I ever became a mother, I will strive to be the best I can. Good enough will not do.

My internal battle is that, despite his tragic story, Wayne is a violent serial rapist. He has terrified innocent women. In order to work with him I have to put that to one side and build a wall in front of what he did. I have to try to see him as a person who did bad things, rather than as a bad person. I suppose I find this easier with him than with some of the others due to his backstory. His faulty patterns of thinking shine through and we have done our job today. As Kenny and I say in our debrief, with his life map Wayne never really stood a chance. It was never going to turn out well for him and I leave the jail that day feeling very sad and hopeless about the world, the human race and how we treat each other.

CHAPTER EIGHTEEN

THERE IS SOMETHING WRONG WITH ME

The next session, Wayne slopes in with a fresh bandage on his forearm and an ashen face. He cannot meet my eyes.

'Sorry, Miss, I've let you down. I've bin puttin' bits of plastic pen in me arm again. I can't help it. I know I'm a fuck-up, I'm sorry.'

I do not know what to say to him. And there is that pattern of thinking again. We have opened up a porthole to his past and it is flooding through. I wonder if we will be able to close it again before he drowns. I feel out of my depth. I do not want to do more damage than good.

We have to carry on and it is Nigel's turn. He has his life map rolled under his arm like it is attached to his armpit with superglue.

'I was expecting to go last, but I'm ready, I suppose. I apologise now for what you've all got to listen to.' He extracts the squashed life map and spreads it out across the floor.

This is Nigel's story:

Here's the joke: I was born on Friday the 13th. I think that's where it went wrong! One of my first memories is of being six and my twin sisters being born. I was very jealous, as they got everything. But I loved them and spent time helping to bath them and stuff for my mam. There was an awful accident with one of them: she fell into the fire when she had just learnt to walk. She was very badly burnt and disfigured, and I felt like it was my fault as I was supposed to be watching them. My mam blamed me and said I was good for nothing. And I was bullied at school about my teeth – every single day, I was mocked. I was so ugly. Even the teachers would call me names.

At puberty I noticed there was something else different about me, apart from my teeth. I was very small down there. I know I am different and there is something wrong with me. I was teased and bullied by the other lads for that too, and preferred talking with the girls at school, when they would let me (which wasn't very often), and my younger sisters at home. I still helped out a lot with them for my mam. Dad wasn't really around. He had a girlfriend. My mum just put up with it. I preferred being around the girls anyway. I started getting aroused when I saw the girls in the bath or running around the house naked. This was all I could think about when I went to bed at night and did what growing boys do. The thing is, as I grew up, this thing did not. I just kept liking younger girls. I don't know why. Was I born like this? What is wrong with me?

Out of the corner of my eye, I can see Sid nodding.

'Yep, that's how it feels, pal. I'm with you. It never goes away, trust me. Got to "manage it" – that's what they taught me at Albany.'

'It's gone away a bit, now I'm in prison.'

'It will, pal, cos you don't see any children, but it bounces back once you're out, believe me. I've realised I am homosexual now, though, so I think I'll be OK this time. Do carry on, though – what you are saying is really clear, to me anyway.'

Nigel gives one of his rare smiles. He isn't used to praise from the others.

I had two girlfriends in my late teens – I think they were only with me because they felt sorry for me – but I finished with them both before I had to have sex with them. I was too embarrassed. I know I am different. I can't tell anybody. I can't talk about sex or my problems with anybody. Dad was never there. I liked looking at porn magazines and pretending the women were my sisters when they were younger. I liked the ones where the women dressed up as young schoolgirls. I would say that is my favourite age.

I started drinking a lot and I could fit in a bit with lads my age, but I still felt better around young girls than grown-ups. I worked in a factory, like my dad, and met Linda. She wanted to get married, and I went along with it. I want to be the same as other people, even though I know I am not. I was twenty-one and she was eighteen. I didn't really fancy her, but she looked quite young. I was scared of grown women. I didn't know what to say to them and I didn't know what to do in bed. My mam was pleased about the marriage. Sex on the wedding night was the worst night of my life and I know Linda was disappointed. At least I was married and did not have to worry about having sex with other women. I carried on using porn and also started noticing girls on the street and at the school next door to the factory. I even bought Linda a school uniform to dress up in. We had a son, but we never had sex again after that. It was a relief. I was very unhappy, though, and was drinking a lot and thinking about sex with schoolgirls.

There was a job advertised for a boiler man/caretaker at the swimming baths and I got it. It was my dream job as there were young, half-naked girls everywhere. I had to be very careful, but sometimes I had to go into the girls' changing rooms.

Frank's hand shoots up.

'Yes, cheers, Frank, I know – CD … I went in on purpose to see them. It gave me stuff for my fantasies. I was having them every day by then,' Nigel says.

I collected any spare clothing I found and kept the lost property in my office, which was the room where the boiler was. I liked finding lost underwear. I was becoming desperate to have sex and there was so much choice at the swimming baths – girls of all ages. I knew I was a weirdo, but there was no going back. I chose two girls who always hung behind at the vending machines after the school swimming lessons. I could tell they didn't want to go home. Thanks to the Core SOTP, I know I groomed them. I bought them sweeties and then I offered them a ciggie. I told them they had to come to the boiler room for it. Only one came back. I know this is it, the sex I have been thinking about all my life. It isn't going to hurt her. I didn't mean to kill her – she screamed, and I panicked. I did not want her spoiling it. I had to shut her up. I had waited all my life for that moment. Afterwards I hid her body in the boiler room. I was in such a panic; I did not know what to do. I went home and tried to pretend everything was normal, but inside I knew it was all over for me.

He pauses. 'I know there are a lot of CDs there, but I hope that explains to you all why I did it.'

Frank puts his hand down. Sid is nodding and leans in, facilitator style, head to one side, and says, 'What are your patterns of thinking, Nigel?'

'Well, that there is something seriously wrong with me, but, you know, there actually *is*. So it's more of a *fact* than a pattern of thinking. My mam used to say it too. I'm small down there. I've got a size issue.' He points at his genitals.

This appears to flummox Sid, and it does me a bit too. I think about it. There is no way of finding out if he does have physical problems or whether it is his interpretation. Yet our job *is* the interpretation and how that impacted on his offending behaviour. There must be lots of men with a 'size issue', perceived or not, who have never gone on to abuse and kill a child. I explain this to him as best I can. Nigel nods and agrees with me, as usual, but I think the information goes in. Louise keeps saying it is all about planting the seeds – in the end they have to do the work themselves.

'And can you see any other patterns?' asks Kenny.

'Well, I'm not really sure, but maybe I have that victim thing that Wayne's got.'

I wasn't sure about this. 'Group, do you see any evidence of that in Nigel's life map?'

'Nope. Not really. It's more that you think there is something wrong with you and you are different. I think there is something about women, though, and that seems to be a general pattern in this group, doesn't it?' says Colin.

'Well, maybe, yeah,' Nigel mumbles, picking his scalp with his grubby fingers. 'But it's not about getting my own back, like Wayne. I am just scared of them. I don't trust them, or find them attractive, sexually like. They just petrify me. Women are like another species.'

'That sounds like a clear pattern, well done,' says Kenny. 'Let's get that on the flip chart. Anything else?'

'Can't think of anything. I thought I'd have the most patterns, though, with what I've done. Is it wrong that I've only got two?'

'Don't worry about it, Nige, mate,' says Wayne. 'It's me that's the most fucked up round here.'

In the debrief, Kenny and I discuss how difficult Nigel's life map was to listen to, but how clear his offending pathway is. I remember my earlier question to myself on hearing his active account. Why would a married man sexually assault and kill a child? It is starting to slot together, and I hope it is for Nigel too.

'Do you think people are born like it – you know, attracted to children? If so, how can they ever change?' Kenny says. 'Come on, you are the psychologist, Bec.'

I raise my eyebrows at him. 'The nature-versus-nur-ture debate … well, that's been going on for years. I think people may have a proclivity, a genetic weakness if you like, that can be triggered by the environment … or not. Like schizophrenia or depression. I don't think it is all one or the other, though. I'm not sure, really. That's my best answer.'

I wish I knew more, but the research on this issue is still developing and inconclusive. (We are still several years away from the thinking that there may be a biological or genetic basis to paedophilia and that it can be considered as a sexual orientation.)

'He is so sure that he was born like that; how will he ever change if that's how it is? Is it like asking a straight man to be gay?' says Kenny.

'I'm not sure he ever can, but we can help him see it and give him some strategies to manage it … maybe? Sometimes I am not so sure we can help. For some men, life has to mean life, doesn't it?'

'Yeah, it does. Do you believe in the death penalty?'

'No, not really, because it doesn't work, does it? It's not a deterrent, otherwise there would be no murders in Texas and those other American states and countries where it's still legal.'

'I don't either, but what about for people who can't change, who are always going to be a danger to kids? It would put them and us out of our misery. It costs thirty grand a year to keep Nigel in here, and he could be here for another thirty years. And I think about my own girls, and how I would never want him living next door. That thing he said about the knickers, it turned my stomach.

I can imagine what he was doing with them, the dirty old git. We should have asked about that, but I didn't want to hear it. It's tough for me, because my youngest is exactly the same age as Kelly was.'

I think about what Kenny is saying. I am not used to hearing him talk about the men like this; he is always so warm and therapeutic. I do not have children so I can't personally relate. I can't imagine how difficult it must be for the facilitators who have their own young children. How do they ever dress, bath, kiss or cuddle their kids? I know from what Kenny – and Len before him – has said that there is an impact, a change in their perception. I do not support the death penalty, because I believe that deliberately killing someone makes us no better than them. But the argument that Kenny put forward about those men who will never change and who will always be a danger to children or others does shake me a little. Despite it all, though, Nigel is a human being. He is trying to understand his behaviour, and our work is to try to stop him from doing it again. Whether or not he is released will never be up to us.

In my whole career I've only ever come across a very small handful of men – extreme and appalling cases, with no hope, desire or motivation for rehabilitation – who I would have personally given a lethal injection to. And Nigel isn't one of them.

CHAPTER NINETEEN

WE ARE ALL HUMAN

The next session, it's Frank's turn. The men are getting used to the format now and sit ready in their tight circle, rolling cigarettes and waiting for Frank to start.

'I don't know if I have got it roight, Miss,' says Frank.

'I am sure you have done your best, Frank.'

This is Frank's life story:

My mum committed suicide when I was six months old by walking in front of a train. My dad said, 'She always was selfish.' The first thing I remember, though, is my stepmum and my dad arguing. She went on at him all the time, nag, nag, nag. I felt sorry for him. She never stopped. She was very strict with me and my sister. If our hands weren't clean at the table, she would make us soak them in bleach and I would have to scrub my nails 'til they bled. My dad used to go off drinking, and who could blame him? He earned it. I fell out of a tree when I was little and banged my head on a brick wall and was in hospital for ages. I had an operation on my brain but kept having blackouts, and there was something wrong with my head after that – everyone said so. I was sent to a special school. I don't know why. It must have been my head. It's my stepmum's fault; she wants rid of me. Am I stupid? Messed about at the special school with the other thick kids. I only got to come home on a weekend. One weekend I came home, and my stepmum had a new baby. She had put it in my room and moved my things into the garage. I slept out there.

When I got to thirteen Dad showed me his porn collection. I liked it. He told me it was normal, and I could see it anytime. Sex – that's what women are there for. He let me drink his beer. I felt grown up and like he cared. My stepmum still nagged us and was mean. She treated her new baby like a prince. One day my dad hit her just to shut her up. I was glad. She deserved it. It's the male right. She needed shutting up.

I had sex with one of the girls at the special school; it didn't mean anything, and I wanted more. It felt good and made me feel better, like a king. I slept with as many of the girls as I could after that. Me and my mate had a shagging competition – who could get the most girls. We had a list of stuff we had to get 'em to do. I won it. I left school with no exams and my dad got me a job with him, labouring, at the building site. It was bostin'; they treated me like a man. They took me out drinking and we did a Friday-night 'pull a pig' comp – basically shag the ugliest woman in the pub. I would shag any bird. You don't look at the mantelpiece when you are poking the fire. Any hole is a goal. That's all they are good for. Fuck 'em and leave 'em. I'm the man. I need a lot of sex; that's what men need. It was all sleazy. I would go for two or three a night if I could. I would shag birds anywhere. I once shagged a bird in a club – she had her head in the loo. She was pissed and being sick. She is just a slut. I did not give a shit. No commitment. I gave one a slap when she gave me some grief about sleeping with her mate. She deserved it; it's what men do. I went out with my dad drinking a lot. We had man-to-man conversations about women and sex. It got us away from my stepmum. He hit her if she started when we got home. He does as he wants; that's what men do; it's our male right. Men have to be king of the castle.

Frank has stopped talking.

'I'm feelin' bad cos I know from the Core I can't use them words about women – it's wrong – but I've put them in cos that's how I saw it then. That's roight, innit, Miss? I would never say "bird" now, or any of those other things. I don't think like that no more.'

I am shocked by Frank's honesty and the extent of his misogynistic attitudes to women. But honesty is what we have asked for.

'That's right, you've done what we asked. What did these early experiences teach you about women and sex, do you think?'

'Well, they were just there for shagging – sorry, sex. I thought they was all sluts, and I didn't care,' he says with a shake of his head.

'What about the use of violence against women?'

'Well, I thought they deserved it; they was all bitches.'

'It looks like something that was modelled by your dad, Frank, is that right?' offers Sid.

'Well, if that's one of your fancy Albany words to mean moi dad showed me how to treat women, you're roight. I thought nothing of hitting them or treating them badly. AT THE TIME!' he bellows. 'Anyhows, it got worse ...' and he continues.

I got a girlfriend and she nagged me to move in together, so I did it to get away from my stepmum. I kept the garage though. I still had my own little fuck palace out there. Bed, TV, porn, fridge for my beer. And I was still shagging other birds. (OLD THOUGHTS.) It wasn't long before she was nagging at me just like my stepmum, and then I found out she was seeing someone behind my back. The stupid fucking bitch, they are all the same. What a whore.

She is just like my stepmum. No woman can be trusted. I'd been at the pub with my dad when I found out and I came home and punched her and broke her jaw. She deserved that. I will make her suffer, get my own back. I will do what I want. That will teach her to mess with me. I am a man. I can do what I want.

I went to court for battery and got a female judge and a stretch inside. Fucking typical – another bitch. There is no chance now. Women should not be allowed to be judges; that's a male privilege. Got shown some hard porn in prison. I liked that – make the bitches suffer.

He drops his shorn, lumpy head. 'I can't read anymore, Miss, I feel real bad sayin' this in front of you, Miss. My language was terrible back then. I can't believe them is moi forts, loike.'

'Thank you, Frank. I appreciate your honesty, and I know we are looking at who you were back then, not now. Don't worry, it's fine. Please carry on.'

I got out of the nick and went to live with Dad. He had split up with me stepmum, at last. We had a bostin' time, the two of us. We even shared a bird one night. I met another girl, Carol. She had a kid already and her own house. She was all roight to start with. She used to let me stay over on a weekend. She didn't like me going out with my dad or my mates drinking.

She would nag me. It was starting all over again. She went away for the weekend. I was glad. I had enough of her constant nagging and rules.

He says the next bit without looking at me.

She wouldn't let me have sex before she went. I needed to empty my ball bag. I was in a bad place. I hated my stepmum, Carol was doing my head in, I hated that female judge. All these women ruining and running my loife. I am the man. I am going to show them who is boss around here.

I went drinking with my dad and borrowed his car and went to pick up a prossie. I needed a shag. I didn't have enough money and she refused me sex. I thought, I'm having a shag, it's my birthright. I'm the king. I am getting what I want, come what may. I had sex with her anyway (AND I KNOW IT'S RAPE NOW), and then she said she was going to the police. The stupid whore, she's gonna tell, I'll go back to jail. I am gonna have to stop her from telling. Carol will find out. I know I said it was a red mist before, and it was. I was angry, I'd been drinking, but now I really think about it, I had these thoughts too. I meant to do it. And so, I killed her, strangled her. It was over quickly, and then you know the rest with the shovel and the grave. I was panicking and just trying not to get caught.

He pauses, then says: 'And I've got moi patterns as: "I will take and do what I want (I am king)", "It's my birth-right (sex)", "Women can't be trusted, they are all bitches and whores" and "I will get my own back and make them suffer". Is that roight, Miss?'

Jeremy looks like he is going to fall off his chair at these insights.

'That *is* right, those are really clear patterns. You have worked really hard, Frank. I'm proud of you.'

And I am. As much as it is unpleasant to listen to, and his offence is appalling, I think about how much Frank has changed since I first met him. He now acknowledges the rape and intent to murder, but it is about far more than getting an admission. Frank's story makes sense to him and us. I can see how his attitudes to women and sex (passed on by his dad and embedded by the pornogra-phy), the sexual frustration and entitlement to sex he felt, the disinhibition that comes with alcohol and the loss of control all combined together in a pot, like some appall-ing recipe, ended in rape and murder. What strikes me is how strong his negative thoughts had been about women and yet he seems very protective now and keen to please me. The two do not fit. I wonder if he has really changed or whether those thoughts are still there, lurk-ing beneath the surface.

* * *

'Do you think he is having us on?' I ask Kenny in the debrief. 'How can all those awful thoughts just disappear? They've been entrenched since childhood, thanks to his dad.'

'I know, but, yes, I do think he has changed. Frank is so honest, and he just says it as it is. I know any of them can be pulling the wool over our eyes, but I don't think Frank is one of them. He's a case where we've made a difference.'

'I hope so, Kenny, it's hard to know. We are not infallible, are we? I think I get a sense when they are lying, or when things don't make sense or fit, but at the end of the day we only have their word for it, don't we?'

Colin is the last group member to present his life map.

'It's the teacher in me,' he remarks as he rolls it out across the floor, and we pull our chairs in. It is very neat and organised, with little drawings dotted about and perfectly joined-up handwriting, like he is presenting to a class of primary school children just learning to write. 'I like to do things well.'

This is Colin's story:

So, I was born into a 'normal family'. Dad was a teacher and Mum stayed at home with me. They were good parents, and I was never abused. I was an only child and had all the attention growing up. When I was seven, Mum went back to work as a nurse. She used to work lots of shifts, and I missed her a lot. I wanted her attention, but she was always too tired for me when she got home. Dad was very strict, but he never beat me or anything. Nan got poorly and Mum used to go and help her. That meant I barely saw her at all and was stuck at home with Dad. I did well at school and worked hard. I loved it when Mum came to watch me in the school plays when she had time.

'What did you learn about the world from these early experiences, Colin?' I ask.

'That I have to work hard. That family is really important.'

'What did you learn about yourself?'

'That I liked attention. That I had to work hard at school. That I can't fail or let Dad down.' He then goes on with his story:

I had a couple of girlfriends growing up, but I did not take them home. Dad was too strict and had high standards. I knew I could not fail my O or my A levels. Dad expected the very best from me. I got good grades. He expected me to go into teaching, so I applied to teaching college, even though I did not really want to go. I got in. He mapped out my life. I still lived at home with Mum and Dad and was still a virgin. But life was OK. I do not have any bad experiences – well, nothing that would point to what I later did.

One day I met Jackie at the bus stop outside college. She was really nice. She was a fair bit older than me and had a daughter, Ellie, aged eight. I started seeing Jackie in secret as I knew Dad would not approve. He still thinks he is in charge, but one day I will have my own life. I fell in love with Jackie, and we had a good sex life – just normal stuff, missionary position. I did not use porn. I did not beat her. We just had a good, normal relationship and I saw her every day at college. I finished college and got a job teaching. I hated it; it was stressful, and the children did not respect me. I knew I could not leave. That would be seen as a fail-ure. But everything else in my life was good and normal.

'You appear to be saying that a lot, that it was all normal,' offers Jeremy. 'Why is that?'

'Good question,' Colin says. 'Well, it's just that it was. I've done the Core. I've heard the horrible lives that people have had – been abused; awful, traumatic things, and that explains their offending. But with me there really isn't anything. It was normal. No abuse. Just normal and a normal relationship.'

'I see,' says Jeremy. 'I wasn't abused either, but I can see now from my life map that there were all sorts of relevant things going on that explain what happened. It doesn't have to be abuse, does it? It's just about the way you are interpreting things at the time. For example, there is this whole thing about your dad and not failing and keeping Jackie a secret. Is that relevant?'

Kenny and I are giving exaggerated nods at Jeremy's insightful question, and I can see Sid doing it too.

'I suppose so – he had high standards and it did put pressure on me not to fail and keep secrets. If you'll let me carry on, it might become more obvious. I'm looking for some answers today. Answers I've never really had,' says Colin.

So, Jackie and I kept seeing each other and Mum and Dad found out. Mum was fine, but Dad says she wasn't good enough for me. For once, I am doing it my way. It's my life. I moved out from my parents and in with Jackie. I will have to make this work. I cannot fail. I will show him I can run my own life.

'How do you see the world and your dad at this point in your life?' asks Sid.

'That you have to work hard, and you can't fail at things you have started. Also, I was starting to push back against Dad. I was starting to do things my way and that felt good – powerful even. That all might be relevant to my offending, I suppose.'

'Could be, pal.'

Things were great with me and Jackie for a year or so, before we got married, and I tried with Ellie. I loved all the attention I got from both of them. Ellie would make me cards at school for Father's Day and my birthday, as her dad had disappeared. I loved it. Jackie would cook a pie and put my name on the pastry. Things cannot be any better. I have everything I want. Then her ex-husband turned up one day and he wanted access to Ellie.

Who do you think you are, coming in here and taking my life? This is my life, not yours – you gave it up. I am going to show you who is in charge around here, and it's not you. Jackie's ex took her to court for custody and it was really stressful. She was preoccupied with him and the court case and she didn't want sex anymore. She stopped making pies. She has stopped giving me the attention I deserve. I am paying for the solicitor, the least she can do is spend some time with me, and notice I am here.

'That's how you felt about your mum, isn't it? You felt like you deserved her attention,' asks Sid. 'The mother–son relationship is crucial. We covered all that at Albany.'

'I think we are all a bit sick of hearing about Albany,' replies Colin. 'But yes, you are right, I did want attention from Jackie and Ellie, and I wanted it from my mum too. I'd sort of spotted that pattern already.'

'Sounds like it is more than "want" attention,' says Sid.

'OK, I thought I deserved it. I was entitled to it, and I wasn't getting it.' He carries on.

I started spending more time with Ellie. She hadn't changed and we got on really well. She wasn't bothered about seeing her dad. I was her dad now. I bought her everything she wanted. People used to say she was the most spoilt kid on the street. I felt closer to her than to Jackie. It is like we have the relationship, not me and Jackie.

He interrupts himself to say, 'Put your hand down, Frank. I know you can't have a relationship with a child, but that is how it felt at the time. And I can see that is where I made my first mistake.' Then he gets back to his story.

One night as I was putting Ellie to bed, as Jackie was too busy, I touched her. That was it and the abuse just went on from there. I knew it was wrong, but she made me feel so loved. Jackie wasn't interested in me anymore. I missed the sex. Jackie's mother was ill now, and between that, the court case and her work, there was no time for me. I hated work, and no, I never offended there before you ask again. I knew I could not let the marriage fail, so I put a brave face on and carried on the abuse. It made me feel better, important. We had a really special relationship.

'That's a CD – well, there are several actually, and there's the failure theme again,' says Jeremy. 'I think it's something you need to consider – just giving you the benefit of my experience here.'

They are like a pair of boxers sparring at the gym, but Colin acquiesces this time.

'Thank you, Jeremy. I suppose I've always felt like I can't fail, always have to keep the standards up. It became a game, hiding it from Jackie, but everything was at stake: my marriage, my job, my relationship with my dad, my reputation, the am-dram club, snooker club. I couldn't let it all go. Everything had to look normal.' He carries on.

The more I did it – the abuse – the more I became obsessed with Ellie. It was happening every day. Then Ellie hit puberty and got a boyfriend. She brought him home one day and they went to her bedroom and shut the door. I was insanely jealous. I need to know what is happening – it's my house – she belongs to me – I'm going to call the shots here. I drilled a spyhole behind the bathroom mirror into her bedroom and I would watch her having sex with her boyfriend and get really angry, but also really aroused. My abuse of her got worse. I was violent and cruel, and I took my anger out on her. Jackie had been my only sexual partner and there were things I wanted to try. I made Ellie do really degrading things to me and to herself, and the more disgusting and humiliating it became, the more aroused I was. I punished her for everything: her mum, her own sexuality, my job, the ex, the situation I was in. I just took it all out on her. The more she became upset, the more I enjoyed it. Soon I couldn't become aroused by just normal sex – well, I know it was rape – with her; it had to be violent and depraved. I became a monster; I know I did.

When she was sixteen, after nearly six years of abuse, she finally told her mum. I was arrested at home with all the neighbours watching. The shame was horrendous. On the outside I was a teacher with a respectable life, an upstanding member of the community. On the inside it was all a sham. I felt like such a failure. I lost everything. The worst day of my life was Dad finding out. I got a long sentence, which I deserved, but I put Ellie through the trial, which I regret. I denied it all until Dad died last year. The same day I put in an app [application] for SOTP. It was like I was waiting until he had gone before I could finally admit it. You see lots of men in here doing the same. They won't admit their offending because they are afraid – they will lose their wives and families. I can't blame those men, but I've got nothing to lose and I am better for getting all this off my chest.

I will never offend again.

Colin takes off his reading glasses and gives them a polish on his shirt. I can see a few of the men nodding.

'Admitting it is easy compared to this, though,' says Wayne. 'This is the most difficult thing I've ever done.'

'What patterns can you see throughout your life then, Colin?' Jeremy asks.

Sometimes I feel like the group can run itself; we are surplus to requirements.

'Well, after what we've said today, there is something about "I cannot fail" and "I deserve attention". It is making more sense to me now. I can guarantee now, I will never reoffend.'

'Anything else?'

'No, I think that's it.'

'Are you sure? I think you've missed something about calling the shots – I'm using your own words there, Colin,' Jeremy says.

'Yes. I was just coming to that actually, there is. I'd spotted that myself. I want to call the shots – be in control, if you like. I needed to be like that to stop it all falling apart. And my offending became more and more controlling as it went along. The stuff I made her do, I can barely think about it. This stuff about your thinking patterns, they need to teach this stuff in schools.'

'Thankfully, I don't think you'll be going near a school again in your lifetime,' Jeremy says.

'Right then,' says Kenny, cranking open the Portakabin window so we can breathe, smoke and empty our tea mugs for a fresh cup. The weeds outside on the gravel are like triffids.

'That's them lot sorted. What about you? Have you done your life map?'

'Er, sort of, yes … have you?'

'Yep, but you go first,' he says with one of his finest facilitator smiles.

'Well, you know about my childhood: it was all pretty normal – who do I sound like there? – until my mum left. I don't actually remember much about that bit; I've sort of blocked it out. Hearing the men talking though, it's made me think about how it's affected my outlook and my thinking.'

'In what way?'

'I think what happened made me think and feel that I am not good enough, unlovable in some way. Mothers don't leave, do they? If my own mother didn't love me enough to hang around and see my childhood through, what does that say about me?'

'And how has that affected your behaviour, do you think?'

'Lots of ways. I think that's why I went off the rails in my teens – rebelling, really making myself unlovable, and perhaps testing my dad's love. I think I expect that everyone I get into a relationship with will leave me.'

'And how does that impact?'

'Well, I don't give all of myself. I keep a bit back. I'm like an ice queen – even Bronwyn told me that!'

'Do you think that's the self-fulfilling thing, like we were taught on the training?'

'Self-fulfilling prophecy? Maybe … I'm creating the situation where they want to leave, so I end it and then I prove to myself I am right all along. I also like things to go my way. Christ, how many times have we heard that on the group? I see parts of me that are like the men … putting myself first, liking to have control over people and relationships, and pretending I feel guilty when I don't.'

'It's weird, isn't it, seeing that we are like them in so many ways?'

'Yeah, it is, but we are all just human, aren't we? And most of us have something in our cupboards. It's not like they have two extra heads or anything,' I say, finishing my tea and watering the weeds with the dregs.

As I walk to the staff tearoom, sandwiched between the red-brick wing and a towering mesh fence, I become aware of an object hurtling towards me. Reflex action makes me duck and shield my head in my hands. There is a resounding slap as the missile lands next to me on the narrow walkway. It is a pigeon. With its head ripped off.

Vivid red, sticky blood has splashed onto my shoe and flicked across the concrete floor and up the fence. My eyes are drawn to the still-flapping bird. I can see the white tip of the spinal column poking out of its body like those twisted iron rods out of cement foundations.

'Whore!' comes a shout from above. I glance up in the general direction of the voice and the four storeys of anonymous barred windows look back, like rows of stealthy eyes. I have no idea which cell it came from.

'Slut!' comes the same angry voice.

I have no choice but to keep walking before something else unpleasant comes my way. I have heard the stories of potting (faeces/urine being collected and thrown at staff). Thankfully the pigeon didn't hit me and thank goodness I did not scream. I force myself not to run, not wanting to appear scared, and try to maintain my dignity. Someone has it in for me – perhaps I have written a negative parole report (at that point I'd never actually written one recommending release; it's so rare to release from a maximum-security prison) or maybe it is a man who just hates women. I know there are plenty of them about.

CHAPTER TWENTY

SCHEMAS

'So today, group, we're going to play a game,' I say. We have the windows as wide open as possible (about 5cm), and the afternoon sun is streaming through into our little box. Through the hovering dust motes, I see Jeremy roll his eyes at Colin. Kenny tips a bag of spectacles out onto the floor. We have been out shopping down the infamous high-street slope to one of the pound stores and elicited a strange glance from the rotund till assistant as we piled numerous pairs of comedy plastic glasses onto the belt. She beeped them through without a word.

'What do you all understand by the expression "seeing the world through rose-tinted glasses"?' I ask.

'Well, it means seeing the world in a more positive way than it really is,' answers Jeremy.

'Thanks, Jeremy, spot on,' Kenny says. 'As we saw on the life maps, we all have different thinking patterns, ways of seeing the world, that developed as we grew up.

Psychologists call these "schemas",' he says, sliding his eyes to me.

'Yes,' I say. 'And another way of thinking about schemas is seeing them as a pair of glasses with tinted lenses. When we put them on, they colour how we see the world. We each have several pairs and the glasses we put on depends on the situation and how we are feeling. Schemas, or glasses, can be about ourselves, others or the world in general. And we all have them.'

'This is confusing me,' says Frank, eyebrows scrunched.

'Me 'n' all,' says Wayne.

'Well, I feel like we are only just getting to the psychology of it all. Finally,' says Jeremy. 'So, I have developed these schemas, as you call them, across my life, based on what has happened to me?'

'That's right, and your schemas have developed as a result of how you *interpreted* the things that happened to you. That's what we were looking for on the life maps,' I say.

'I see. It made me the person I am,' Jeremy says.

'That's right.'

'And I still have the patterns now?'

'We all have them, Jeremy, everyone in this room. They help us deal with our lives. Help us understand what is happening to us. When we go into a situation, we try to make sense of it. It's what humans do. We use our schemas, or our glasses, as we are calling them on this group. They are triggered, or "go live", by everyday situations.'

'I see,' says Jeremy. 'I really do. I have been waiting for this!'

He gives me a smile and I smile back.

'I think we might have done something like this at Albany …' says Sid.

'How do they relate to offending?' asks Colin, interrupting him and sitting forward in his chair.

'Excellent question, Colin. The problem is, these glasses or schemas can be unhelpful sometimes. They can colour how we see the world and lead to unhealthy behaviours. We are going to be thinking about what your schemas might be and how they led to your offending.'

'I'm still a bit lost, Miss,' says Frank.

'It's complicated stuff, Frank, and this is all new to you. Don't worry, we are going to play a game now and hopefully that will help.'

'Do we have to play the game? I get it. I just want to know what my schemas are,' says Jeremy.

'I know you do. We'll play the game so everyone can understand. Perhaps you can go first so you can help the others.'

'Of course,' Jeremy says, with another proud smile.

'So, you are going to put on a pair of glasses, which will colour your world, as if a schema has been activated or "gone live". I will tell you what the schema is in secret, but the rest of the group have to try to guess it by asking you questions. OK?'

Jeremy dons a huge pair of red plastic glasses. I pass him a note with 'I AM USELESS' on it. He glances at it and raises his eyebrows. Immediately he changes his usual rigid stance in the chair and drops his shoulders.

'OK, I'll start,' says Kenny. 'How has your day been so far today?'

'It's been terrible, nothing has gone right so far.'

'Oh dear, why's that?'

'I dropped a pint of milk in my cell. Then I nearly missed the group because I was cleaning it up.'

'How are you getting on in your history degree?' asks Colin.

Jeremy observes me through the big red plastic glasses, eyes slightly distorted. 'Ooh, that's a hard one. That's not how I think.'

'Try to think how you would interpret and answer that question if you did have those schema glasses on,' I say.

'OK, I am not doing very well at my degree. I find it really hard; I am not very good at it. I will probably fail,' says Jeremy in a strained voice.

Wayne is smirking, 'That's not like you.'

'No,' whispers Nigel. 'But you sound exactly like me. I've got a question: why do you think you are doing so badly at your degree?'

'It's because I am useless.'

'That's the schema!' says Nigel. 'I only know because it's mine too.'

'I might have it too,' says Wayne, with a worried glance. 'Or somefin' like it anyhow.'

'That's what we are going to be covering next,' says Kenny. 'Your own schemas.'

He explains that the patterns we identified in the life maps are their schemas. We will be looking at how they relate to their sexual offending and then at how they can be modified and managed. Schemas can 'go live' at any time if they are triggered, and they may put their schema glasses on in the sessions. Our job as a group will be to spot this.

'I don't think I will be able to see mine,' says Nigel.

'There you go, Nigel, you've got them on right now,' says Jeremy.

'Have I?'

'Yes, yours is going to be easy. I think mine might be more complex. Now, is it time for tea?' he says.

'Your whole tea-making, laminate-sheet thing is a schema. Just giving you the benefit of my experience,' says Colin. Jeremy looks at him, the tuft of wayward hair having its own party again.

'Is it? No, I don't think so. I am simply being organised, so I know what everyone is having.'

'Yes, that's the point. Why do you need a laminated sheet for that? It's extreme. You have your schema glasses on when you do it.'

'But it's helpful.'

229

'OK, that's an interesting point,' I say. 'What do you get out of having the sheet, Jeremy?'

'Well, as I say, organisation.'

'Why is that important to you?' I ask.

'Well, it keeps everything in order, in control,' he answers.

'Is that a pattern of thinking that you identified from your life map? About keeping things in control?'

He looks at me like all the pennies in his slot machine have suddenly dropped at once.

'Oh my God, yes, I *do* like things to be organised and under control.'

'Can you think of examples in your past life where this was operating?' I ask.

'Yes, all the time. The police, the order, the rules.'

'OK, great examples. And in your sexual offending?' I am pushing it now, but he is on a roll and so am I.

'The planning and everything, perhaps? I need to think about it some more. I will make some notes on it for the next session.'

'There you go again,' says Colin. 'The whole making-notes thing. You are doing it again. You've got your schema glasses on. Nobody else makes notes. That's you and wanting to be in control all the time. Just roll with it for once.'

Jeremy looks alarmed at the concept, and Sid nods, head to one side, a *Mona Lisa* smile gently pinned to his face.

'You are exactly the same, Colin – you like being organised. You had all your patterns written down in the life maps. It's because we are professionals,' says Jeremy.

Colin smiles his teacher's smile. 'Or maybe I just have that schema too?'

'So, coming back to what Colin says. Do you think your organised tea-making might be your schema glasses?' Kenny asks.

'Well, it might be, but it's not a bad thing, is it? Who wants to get the wrong tea?' he says, standing up and getting on with the job.

'So, Becky, what are your schemas?' asks Kenny as we debrief over a fresh mug of tea and a couple of leftover biscuits.

'Well, as I said when we looked at my life map … I might have something about control … maybe "no one messes with me" sums it up?'

'Why is that important?'

'I don't like people messing with me! I need to be the one with the upper hand.'

'Why?'

'To stop myself getting hurt, I guess. It's what I did with my mother. Tried to shut it all off, the feelings of abandonment and rejection. No one messes with me. If I keep people at arm's length, then I don't get hurt. It's all about control. I'll have a think about the others, but I'm worried I share a schema with Jeremy.'

'Maybe that's why you've spent two years rubbing each other up the wrong way.'

As usual, I think Kenny is spot on. He should be a psychologist.

CHAPTER TWENTY-ONE

SCHEMA MODIFICATION

'I killed to take control,' says Jeremy. 'I have been thinking about your question about how my schemas fit with my offending. Needing to be in control explains it all. The way I planned it. Carried it out. Killed the dog walker. It all fits. There are so many examples in my life of needing to show I am the best, being in control, thinking that emotion is a sign of weakness. They are my three strongest. I think I have "women are a different species" as well … I have written them all down here, colour-coded across my life so you can all see it.'

He hands out neatly written sheets showing the development of his schemas over his life and culminating in the offence.

'And, before you say it,' he says, looking at Colin and Sid above his new reading glasses, 'I know this is an example of my control schema. But this is it operating in a good way. Isn't that what you say, Rebecca, that sometimes it can work for us?'

'That's right. Our schemas developed to help us make sense of the world. Sometimes they are helpful. It's about learning when they are dysfunctional and not being helpful for either ourselves or others. Can you give us an example of when your schema is not helpful?'

'Well, yes, my offending, obviously.'

'What about in everyday life?'

'If you are going to go on about the tea again, I have said, who wants the wrong tea?'

'How might others see that behaviour?'

'Well, it's just me making the tea. Crikey, why are you making such a big deal about the flipping tea? I'm in here for rape and murder.'

'Let's ask the group.'

'It sets you up to look like you are better than us. That's your schema. You need to show that you are superior in every situation. Do you think you are better than us?' says Sid.

Jeremy hesitates.

'Well …'

'He thinks he is better than me,' says Wayne. 'He's said that all along. Well, you're not, Jeremy. You raped a woman and killed a fella. You're no better than me, man. Don't matter whether you was a copper or not.'

'I know I do that. I am thinking more about my higher education and lack of criminal career beforehand, but when you say it like that, I can see what you mean. I didn't realise that's how I appear when I am making the tea.'

'So, how can you challenge that schema?' I ask.

'I will let someone else make the tea?'

'It's about challenging the thoughts that lead you to do it. If you can practise getting the schema under control for the little, everyday things, then this will help with the bigger issues, including those that led to your offending.'

'I am good at getting things under control, as you know, Rebecca,' he says with a little smile. 'OK, so my self-talk will be: *this is my schema, I am trying to control the situation. I can't make the tea. Let someone else do it.*'

'Let's try it – it's break time. Let's do an experiment.'

Jeremy sits back with a sigh and Colin stands up to make the tea. I can see Jeremy clenching his fists as Colin fumbles with the cups, ignoring the laminated sheet and asking everyone what they want.

'How's it going, Jeremy?' asks Kenny.

'Well, he is not referring to the sheet. I don't put the milk in first and he is doing it all wrong, but I am trying to stop my thoughts and remember where my need to control has led in the past. Rape and murder. Perhaps I can do a rota so that everyone can take a turn at the tea-making?'

I try to control the horror on my face.

'*Joke*, Rebecca. Got you there, didn't I!'

* * *

After the sub-standard tea, we move on to Wayne. We want to work with his schema about how he sees himself and how this fits with the rapes.

'I raped the women cos I was trying to get my own back,' says Wayne. 'I thought women were all the same and when I did it, the rapes and all the other stuff, I felt powerful and in charge for once in my life. That's another one. I've got five patterns, more than anyone else. My other schemas are no one cares and I'm no good, a big fuck-up. And that's true. I don't care what any of you say. I've raped lots of women and I got life. I deserve to die in prison. How can you say I'm not a fuck-up?'

'A difficult one, pal – you have fucked up, no doubt about it. We all have,' says Sid.

Six pairs of searching eyes turn to Kenny and me.

'It sounds like you might have your glasses on now, Wayne,' I say.

'Yeah. I fink I have.'

'I wonder if we can think about whether there are any times that you don't have those glasses on.'

'I have always got them on. It's like I say, I'm a big fuck-up.'

'Group, can you help Wayne, please? The thing about these schemas is, it's really hard for the person to see that there might be a different way of thinking. That the belief is not the absolute truth all of the time,' I say.

The group is silent until Colin says, 'You are here. You finished the Core SOTP. You are doing the

Extended Programme. That's not a fuck-up, that's you taking responsibility and trying to change yourself.'

'S'pose.'

'Are you trying to change yourself, pal?'

'Definitely, Sid, all I think about, but I am no good at nothing, never 'ave bin.'

'How does you wanting to change and doing the programmes fit with you being no good at anything?' I ask.

'I'm doin' all right at this … sometimes. When I understand it.'

'Let's ask the group. You don't sound too sure.'

'You are doing great,' says Sid. 'It's a very hard thing, to come into therapy. I have noticed you are very honest and very sorry.'

Wayne looks like he could weep.

'And you have helped me loads with my life map and stuff,' says Frank, ever eager to please.

'You are doing far better than me,' says Nigel. 'Oh, hang on, that might be my schema.'

'It might be, Nigel, but hold that thought. So, Wayne, how does it feel to hear that?'

'Feels weird.'

'Do you think they are making it up?'

'No …'

'So, how do those comments fit with you being no good all of the time?'

'They don't.'

'So, is it possible that some of the time you do OK?'

'S'pose so, in the group, yeah.'

'So, what does that tell you about the schema?'

'I'm OK in the group?'

'Well done, Wayne. That is the first time in two years I have ever heard you say anything positive about yourself. We know that schema is linked to your offending. Let's have a think about some self-talk so that in the future, when that schema goes live, you can challenge it.'

Colin wants to work on his 'I cannot fail' schema, which is interesting, as we want to work on his 'I need to call the shots' (control) schema. He is insistent that the schema he wants to work on is the most important.

'Colin. You've got the glasses on,' says Jeremy. 'Here you are, trying to call the shots about working on your "I need to call the shots" schema. It's so ironic it's incredible.'

'What do you think about that, Colin?' I say. 'Jeremy does have a really good point here. Have you got your schema glasses on?'

Jeremy inclines his long neck, as if he is about to be knighted, and gives me his 'you are very welcome' look.

'Well, if that's what you all think is the most important, let's do that then. And maybe I do have the glasses on, Jeremy, you are right … er … just this once.'

'Great. So, remind us how this schema fits with your life and offending,' says Kenny.

'I felt like I needed to call the shots and be in charge of my own life after Dad tried to impose his life on mine. When everything was a mess with Jackie and her ex, I took control back and started offending against her daughter. And all my offences are about being in charge, in command. I had total control of Ellie in the things I made her do and with the spyhole and everything. And I got off on that. I also see it in other parts of my life – I had to be the treasurer at the snooker club, for example.'

'And what about in prison, how is it playing out now?' I ask.

'Well, just now … in the session … possibly?'

'Yep, well recognised. What about your cell?' says Kenny. 'I've seen how that looks …'

'Well, yes, I keep a clean and tidy cell. That's a healthy function of the schema though, surely?'

'I'll agree with you there for once,' says Jeremy.

'What about your budgie?' says Nigel bravely.

'My budgie? What on earth has that got to do with anything?'

'Well, it's the most spoilt budgie on the wing. It's the in-joke, isn't it?' says Nigel.

'I just look after my budgie well. It's about the only privilege us well-behaved lifers get aside from choosing our own quilt covers.'

'That's what people said about your victim, Ellie – wasn't she the most spoilt kid on the street?' says Wayne.

'Roight, I'm getting this now!' says Frank, moving to the edge of his chair.

'So am I, I think …' says Colin. 'I'd not thought of that before. Thanks, Nigel.'

'It's known as offence-paralleling behaviour, pal,' says Sid.

'He learnt it at Albany,' says Wayne, quick as a flash.

'Thank you, Wayne. So, offence-paralleling behaviour is when elements of your behaviour now parallel or reflect those when you were offending. And it's possible, likely even, that the same schema underlies both. Do you think that's a possibility?' I ask?

'I do,' says Colin. 'Although I'm not about to start mistreating my budgie just to prove I'm no longer a risk.'

'We are not asking you to,' I say. 'It's more about recognising that the behaviours may be driven by the same thinking.'

'I think the thing with the budgie isn't really about calling the shots – that's slightly different – but it is about having control over things, liking things neat, having order and power maybe. So yes, I suppose you are all right, it does link with my offending.'

'Well said. Now we need to have a look at helping you with some self-talk and learning to recognise other situations where you may be trying to overly control things or call the shots,' says Kenny. 'Well done, everyone, that was a good piece of work.'

* * *

Of course, these sessions where we try to help the men modify their schemas are incredibly tough. Years of experiences have built over time like sediment forming a rock face. The schema work is like viewing a cross-section of the layers that have built up. We cannot undo the formation. It is set. But we can help them consider whether the schema is an unconditional truth, chipping away at it like we have tiny rock hammers. After we look at how the men's schemas link to their sexual offending, we help them try to identify situations in which the schema may not work for them. We try to help them see a chink of a different way of thinking and develop some alternative self-talk. We get them keeping diaries and doing behavioural experiments in the group and on the wing, trying out the new self-talk and reporting back to the group.

Wayne tells us about trusting a female officer to sort out his canteen when there was a problem. He has always approached the male officers. She fixes it for him (thankfully), and he adds it as one example that goes against his schema that all women are the same and cannot be trusted. He also includes me in his list as a woman that 'wern't that bad even if she is a syco'.

Sid tells us a similar story about trying to talk to the workshop staff and other prisoners. His 'got to keep things a secret/no one wants me/I am a freak' schemas always prevented him from engaging with others. They are good examples, but I am concerned he is impression managing. He is showing us what he wants us to see. I am not convinced he will tell any secrets that will paint him in a bad light.

Frank tells us about how his 'I will take what I want' schema always leads to issues at the servery. He always wants to be first in the queue ('like a king') and to have the best bits of the meat. 'It's dog eat dog in here, but I am not going to starve if I let this new con [convict] in before me, just this once' went his new self-talk. His old 'I will take what I want' schema linked directly to his sexual offending; he was so entitled when it came to sex, he described it as his 'birth right'. If he can work on not taking what he wants in prison, can he work on not taking sex on release?

Nigel, like Wayne, has a very strong 'I am not good enough' schema. The men are constantly picking him up on it. He starts to see it in the sessions for himself – 'There I go again,' he will say. Yet he cannot get over his 'there is something wrong with me' schema. We weigh up the positives and negatives of holding the schema and he can see that it is unhelpful and how it relates to offending, but he still believes it as an absolute truth. Schemas can take years to modify, and we have to leave it with him. It is frustrating, but these men are not easy doer-uppers. Their soup is made, and we cannot take the onions out.

* * *

Not all their experiments and diaries are successful, and they have an uphill battle ahead as convicted sex offenders. Prison officers do not always behave as you would want them to when approached by prisoners who are trying out their new skills. The group members are up against the macho and chauvinistic culture that still reigns supreme. They are exposed to attitudes, beliefs and behaviours that feed and support their faulty schemas instead of helping to modify them. The Programmes Department has started running SOTP awareness sessions to try to make some inroads, educating the staff about collusion and how to provide support to prisoners in treatment. The take-up is low and heckling is common. Daniel enjoys the challenge of running these sessions, but I can't bear the adversarial nature of it and the put-downs. I find the men in the group easier to deal with than some of the staff. The group members are more motivated and open to change.

Prisons are a tough place to rehabilitate. In addition to the sexist backdrop, the threat of violence and the need to keep secrets, stay safe and maintain a reputation, all while watching your back, does not encourage openness, honesty and reform in the men. The group room is their safe place. They keep coming back with their examples, calling each other out when a schema goes live in the group, encouraging each other to challenge it and take off the glasses. The men act like mirrors and see their own schemas reflected in each other. They even report on some of the inappropriate attitudes of the staff and have a good go at identifying some of the officers' defective schemas. I wonder if they have tried to guess mine.

Watching the men battle with their own schemas leads Kenny and I to discuss our own at every opportunity. After my life map session with him, I am able to identify four patterns of thinking – schemas – of my own.

I have an entitlement schema: 'I deserve ...' It's not quite like Frank's, but I think it partly comes from being the oldest sister of three. Sibling order is said to be one of the strongest determinants of personality, and I can see how being the oldest (and never feeling the favourite) led me to thinking that I deserved more or needed to be the first or best at something. This schema is very present throughout my adult relationships.

I have an 'I am unlovable/not good enough' schema not dissimilar to Wayne's and Nigel's, which runs very deep and stems from my mother leaving and me feeling not wanted. If she couldn't love me, who else can or will? I like to keep this one hidden. My vanity and need to always have my nails done is an example of this schema in action. If I look good on the outside, I feel the part on the inside. Validation has to come externally – if other people think I look good, therefore I am.

I have a control schema – 'no one messes with me' – that resembles Jeremy's and Colin's and Frank's. This acts as a defence mechanism and compensates for 'I am unlovable'. It means I keep people at arm's length (then no one can mess with me, and I can't get damaged again).

And finally, Kenny helps me identify that I have a 'people let you down' schema. Again, this stems from my childhood experiences. I expect the worst in people and have problems with trust. It means I struggle to let others in and to show my emotions. I know I can be hard and prickly and resemble Bronwyn's perfectly described 'ice queen'.

It is strange to see that I have similar thinking habits as a bunch of murderers, rapists and child molesters. Surely our thinking should set us apart? Instead, it confirms once again that they are really not all that different. Or maybe I am as damaged as them. Working on our own schemas is as tough for Kenny and me as it is for the men. Ours are just as entrenched, and while not so dysfunctional that we have committed crimes, I sometimes feel like the men are doing better at wrestling with their own faulty thinking than I am with mine.

Jeremy finally lets others make the tea without complaining, although he sits stiff as a corpse while they do it. Frank waits his turn at the servery. Wayne tries to interact appropriately with one female staff member a day, if there is one on duty. These may appear like irrelevant pieces of behaviour, but they are examples of the men challenging their underlying belief system – the same belief system that led them to commit their offences of rape and murder and child abuse.

CHAPTER TWENTY-TWO

ATTACHMENT STYLES

The year is rolling towards Christmas and the days are dank and gloomy. I am at the prison and planning in the group room with Kenny, before the sun – and usually Daniel – struggles out of bed. I do not leave the jail until it is dark again. It feels like my whole world is the Extended Programme. I spend my evenings thinking about the men: how we can confront their schemas, what techniques we can use to help them adjust their thinking or a new behavioural experiment we can try. Daniel is sick of it and says he can't wait for it to finish so he can 'have me back'. He forbids me from talking about it at night and is jealous about the bond I have with Kenny, who is like a big brother to me.

Our little group room never seems to get fully light. One chilly morning in mid-December we gather in our usual chairs. There are elaborate frost patterns scattered across the inside of the Portakabin windows and I can see my breath hanging in the air. We have moved onto the next block of the course, and I have just described attachment theory to the men – that is, how we relate and behave in intimate relationships as adults, is influenced by our early attachments with parents and caregivers. Dysfunctional attachment styles are thought to be related to sexual offending. Children who grow up with warm, boundaried parents learn through this modelling the skills to have positive intimate relationships as adults. Children who grow up with cold, rejecting, inconsistent or abusive caregivers may develop insecure attachment styles and their adult relationships are likely to involve anxiety, avoidance, rejection and/or a fear of sex and intimacy. Intimacy skills are often deficient in sexual offenders, and I know from hearing the men's life maps that they have either been poorly parented, suffered abuse or struggled to have healthy relationships with other consenting adults (or all three of the above).

It is hypothesised that there are four attachment styles; Kenny and I explain that the first attachment style is 'secure'. This means that your view of others is positive and your view of yourself is positive. People with this style tend to have good, supportive intimate relationships.

'Not sure anyone in this room has got that one,' says Frank. 'Well, apart from maybe you, Miss, and you, Kenny. I bet you are both a number one!'

Oh, Frank, if only you knew – I am so very far from that.

We tell them that the number-two attachment style is 'anxious-ambivalent', which describes people who see others as positive and worthy, and themselves as negative. People with this style can be clingy and needy in relationships.

'That's me then,' says Nigel. 'Is that the worst one?'

'Got your glasses on there, Nigel,' says Frank.

'Ah. I know, there I go again,' he says with slumped shoulders. 'I know I am doing it, but I'm just so useless I can't stop.'

After trying to help Nigel take off his glasses again, we move on to the third attachment style, which is 'avoidant-fearful'. This, we tell the men, is when you see yourself in a negative way and others in a negative way. People with this style don't trust partners and fear rejection.

'S'me all over,' says Wayne. 'I've never trusted no one in my life after what happened with me mum. Then me girlfriends all shat on me.'

'Do you think that is because you always expected them to?' asks Jeremy. 'Maybe it was something in your behaviour, you know, because of your attachment style and schemas. You expected them to "shit on you", as you say, so you treat them badly and so they do it.'

'That's called a self-fulfilling prophecy,' says Sid. 'We learnt it at Albany.'

It is Sid. And like Wayne, that's exactly what I do in relationships.

'Wow, you are on fire today, group!' Kenny says.

Jeremy beams. 'It's all this complex psychology,' he says. 'We are finally here. I am finally getting it, all of it. It's so clear to me now why I did it. Why we all did it. I thought I would never know.'

He smiles and his face is open and relaxed, as if someone has steamed all the creases away.

'S'all still confusing me,' says Wayne. 'Are you saying that Shaz did that cos of me? She cheated on me, remember.'

'Yeah, if you expect things to go wrong, you behave in a way that makes them go wrong,' says Sid. 'Don't worry, Wayne, I am a number three too, pal.'

I think I might be too, Sid.

'What's number four?' asks Frank. 'I don't think we have got to me yet.'

We explain that number four is 'avoidant-dismissive'. This describes people who have a positive view of themselves, but in a way that demeans or puts others down. They see others as negative and untrustworthy and can come across as cold and aloof.

'Yep, that's me then,' says Frank.

'And me,' says Colin.

'And me too, I think,' says Jeremy. 'Definitely the cold and aloof bit, although I really do want intimacy so maybe I am a bit of number two as well. Can you be more than one style?'

I explain that people tend to have a predominant

attachment style. This exercise is about helping them understand the typical way they may revert to behaving in relationships, based on how they were parented and what they learnt about relationships as they were growing up. We will be spending the session looking at which attachment style they resemble the most closely and looking at patterns of how they have behaved in previous relationships.

'It's very difficult to put people in boxes, and we don't want to do that,' I say.

'I never seem to fit neatly into your boxes anyway, Rebecca,' says Jeremy.

'What do you think mine is, Bec?' Kenny asks when they have all gone, a concerned look on his face.

'Anxious-ambivalent,' I come straight back with. 'Sorry, that's crap of me. What do you think it is?'

'I think you are right, as ever,' he says with a wide grin. 'I just want to be loved! What do you think yours is?'

'I've been thinking about it … definitely not secure. I can be quite snobby and think I am better than people, but underneath I am not sure I feel deserving of real love. It all comes back to my childhood, again. I push people away. No one messes with me, and all that. So, does that make me a number three? Avoidant-fearful? Oh God, that's the worst one!'

'No, it's not. Mine's far worse than yours.'

'I think you will find that you've got your schema glasses on there, Kenny.'

Later that week Kenny and I are in my office and the weak morning sun is filtering through the bars. I am touching up my nails as I usually do before a session. Groomed on the outside helps with the holes inside. I really need to do something about this behaviour, I tell myself.

'We can wing it a bit again today, can't we, Becky?' Kenny asks.

'Yeah, I think we can, we know what we are doing. It's hard to plan these sessions anyway. You never know what they are going to say and when their schemas are going to go live.'

'Blimey, remember when we started, we could never have said that. We've come a long way.'

'We certainly have,' I say as I answer the ringing plastic phone. 'Rebecca Myers, Higher Psychologist.'

It is the first time I have said my title since my promotion. Kenny winks at me.

'Hullo. It's Elizabeth from Headquarters.'

I put down the nail varnish. Kenny has heard who it is and sits up; Elizabeth's regal presence seeps down the phone line.

'Oh, hello, Elizabeth,' I say in my best phone voice. 'How can I help you?'

'Congratulations on your promotion. We need someone to help deliver the SOTP training, nationally, and we thought of you. Would you be interested? I've spoken to Louise, and she thinks you will be brilliant. She thinks you are one of the best facilitators she has ever seen. And also, I wondered if you will be applying for the national job we advertised, working in my team?'

Me? Apply for 'The Job'? I've seen it advertised and counted myself out as not experienced enough. It is far too high profile. *Run training …? One of the best facilitators …? Surely not. What about Alex Bull and the other experienced psychologists? There must be a mistake. They are going to see that I am actually no good at this underneath it all. I've just been getting away with it all this time.*

'Er … thank you for the offer. I don't know what to say.'

Kenny is nodding so enthusiastically at me that I am worried for his neck.

'Say YES!' he mouths.

'Why don't you have a think about both those things,' says Elizabeth.

After the phone is down, I turn to Kenny.

'Don't you dare say no,' he says. 'Come on, what glasses have you got on now, Becky?'

'I'm not sure I am good enough yet for the national training or The Job. I know I have got them on, but it's a fact.'

'You are good enough and you sound like bloody Nigel! You'd be amazing at both those things, although I'd bloody miss you. We are winging these sessions. You are an expert at all this. Take your glasses off! And maybe next time I can come with you on the training, cos she didn't ask me, did she?'

'Now who's got their glasses on?'

CHAPTER TWENTY-THREE

SEX AND RELATIONSHIPS

After identifying the men's attachment styles, we move on to exploring their old relationship patterns, the role of sexual fantasy in their offending and how their schemas and attachment styles played out in their relationships. Then we help them practise new intimacy skills for communicating about sex and jealousy, for conflict resolution, managing and expressing their emotions and perspective taking. I feel like we are trying to grow new men out of the old ones, like potatoes. The group enters the New Year, which feels symbolic. The reasons why the men committed their offences become even clearer, like a tricky jigsaw puzzle finally coming together to reveal the final picture.

Jeremy can see how his older parents' lack of emotions and demonstrative intimacy taught him that having feelings and showing love is awkward and uncomfortable. His first sexual experience at the cinema was humiliating, teaching him that women cannot be trusted, that sex is embarrassing and emotions painful. He was unable to form intimate relationships with adults – he did not have the skills and was afraid of opening up. He talked about how he hoped the victim would fall in love with him and teach him about sex. He fantasised about this with increasing frequency in the build-up, convincing himself that the offence was a 'date'.

He wants to practise 'feeling' emotions and reports to us that he has been watching programmes about the homeless, 'tearjerker' films about romance and reading books about the Holocaust and people with terminal illness. We admire his commitment, and he always comes to the sessions with a full, neat diary of his attempts at finding his 'hidden emotions'. Colin will roll his eyes and challenge him about his cognitive and organised approach to what is supposed to be an emotional task.

Colin's parents also did not show love and his dad was controlling and had high expectations of him. Like Jeremy, he had never practised sexual relationships in his teens and craved attention in his first adult relationship, learning to equate sex with love. When his relationship started to break down and he was unable to talk to his partner, he became lonely and sexually frustrated, seeking attention and intimacy from his victim. The abuse became cruel and sadistic, partly out of an attempt to punish his wife, but Colin also admitted that he enjoyed this type of sex. He had always wanted to try different sexual activities with his wife, but she was not interested – or rather, he did not know how to ask her, he now acknowledges. Each time he abused the victim in a cruel way, it reinforced his behaviour, and he became more and more violent in an attempt to satisfy his urges. We run role plays to help him practise talking to a possible future partner about sex, using Kenny as his partner, as no one else will volunteer.

With help from the group Frank can see that he felt rejected and unwanted by the two key caregiving women in his early years: his mum and stepmum. This shaped his early beliefs about women. Frank explores how he learnt his derogatory attitudes about women and sex from his dad and by witnessing the domestic violence at home. Also, that pornography and the culture he worked in played a role in his misogynistic beliefs. Sex was always about him and his needs. He also liked to have sex when he was angry, to soothe himself, and was preoccupied on a daily basis by getting sex, seeing it as his right as a man. While not experiencing explicit rape fantasies, he would masturbate when angry and he could see that the sex he thought about was solely focused on him and ignored consent and the wishes of the woman. He worries that he might have raped women before, because he never asked for consent and 'treated them loike pieces of meat with a hole or three'. We talk about the sort of relationship he would like to have if he ever gets released and what consent is. Not many of the men really seem to know the basics. He practises expressing his emotions to a partner in a role play, getting over the embarrassment of the task to try to 'get it roight'.

Nigel finds these sessions very difficult but admits to a continuing interest in young girls and having sexual fantasies about them, which is hard to hear. We know he has been caught cutting pictures of children out of mail-order catalogues and hand drawings of children have also been found in his cell. From the life-map work we have already helped him work out how his interest developed. Due in part to his perception/the fact that he has a small penis and his worries about his teeth, he is scared of adult women and thinks they will laugh at him. When offending, he thought that a child would not laugh or humiliate him, and that he would finally feel adequate when he was with them. Fantasies about having sex with children made him feel better about himself and the thought of having sex with a child became the only way he thought he could be fulfilled. While he initially had the capacity to have an interest in adult women, and have a son, it is obvious that his clear preference is for female children. This is a difficult one for the group to deal with. He has no desire to have a relationship with an adult. He says his best hope is an over-age, young-looking woman dressed as a schoolgirl. He likes Britney Spears as she dresses as a schoolgirl in her music video. 'And she is sixteen! So, it's legal!' he insists.

It's all I could think about when I saw Britney in that video: how it just wasn't going to help men like Nigel. We discuss how, while not breaking the law, the fantasies, the cuttings, the drawings are all offence-related behaviours and may be strengthening his interest in young girls. I felt like we are stuck with absolutely nowhere to go, and the group do too.

Wayne's sexual abuse by his mother, and other carers, the violent abuse by his stepfather and the witnessing of domestic and sexual violence as a child have taught him that the world is an unsafe place. He is fearful of sex and others, especially women, and places no value on his own self. He admits to masturbating to rape fantasies about his mother throughout his teens, and these became very intense prior to his sexual offence against her. Wayne used sex as a coping mechanism and his rape fantasy, where he took revenge and held ultimate control, made him feel better about himself, like a medicine. The offences were an outpouring of his pent-up anger towards women. It is these fantasies that drove the repeat offending. He is embarrassed and confused that he abused others when he knows the damage of abuse first-hand. Wayne also talks about the thrill he achieved when he offended and made women feel shocked or scared. It is this feeling that drove his indecent exposures in the community and prison, as well as his index offences. Wayne is lost in the relationship skills role plays, but he sticks with them. He wants another chance at life and at relationships. He does not know if he deserves it after the damage he has caused to his victims.

One session he comes into the group with a smile as wide as a crater.

'Miss, I've been on a visit!'

'I thought you look pleased with yourself. Who came to see you?'

'Me sister. I've not seen her in years, but I got Jeremy to help me write her a letter.'

The whole group looks at Jeremy, who is matching Wayne's smile with a broad one of his own.

'Oh, well done. And … er … thank you, Jeremy,' I say. 'And how did the visit go?'

'It were excellent, Miss. I practised all me new skills and told her how I was feeling, and even told her a bit about me offending and why I did it. And at the end, I asked her for a quick hug.'

Kenny and I look at each other and smile, like jubilant parents.

'It's the first time in me life I've *ever* asked anyone for a hug. In fact, it might of bin the first proper hug I've ever had from me family. And it were strange, but it were really nice.'

I blink quickly as my eyes start to fill and a lump the size of a small walnut appears at the top of my throat. His first ever hug.

'Fantastic, Wayne, I'm so very proud of you.'

'Me too,' says Kenny. 'We all are.'

Sid, despite telling himself that his own abuse has caused no harm, can acknowledge that he must have been very confused at the time. He now knows that the abuse he experienced as a boy was wrong, but he used to get an erection while it was happening and cannot reconcile the two.

'They told me at Albany, that's just the body's physical response, but I can see now how it is all confusing to a young boy. And then I learnt to keep everything and sex a secret.'

Sid thought he was gay from a young age but was frightened to admit it at the time. 'It had not long been legal.' He was scared of adult women and has never found a female attractive. Masturbating in secret to young boys made him feel better, and each time he masturbated or offended it reinforced his interest.

'I did some special treatment at Albany for my sexual interests.'

Nigel sits up. 'A cure?'

'Not a cure, sorry, pal. All about managing the urges, as they say at Albany. The treatment is called behaviour modification, I think. It's nothing to do with those injections. Basically, they gave me this stuff in a bottle that stunk of pee, really bad. It's called ammonia and the smell of it hurts your head and nostrils. I had to pair this with thoughts of boys, whenever I had them. They do lots of work like this at Albany, and smelling it just put me off straight away. It seemed to work when I used it, but they took it off me when I came to this jail. Shame. Anyway, I've acknowledged my homosexuality now and would like to have a relationship with an adult man. He will need to be quite young-looking, though – say about twenty.'

'You're in your sixties, though, Sid,' says Colin. 'Isn't that offence-related, like we said about Nigel?'

'Well, it's not breaking the law, is it? As long as it's consenting then it doesn't matter, does it?'

Everyone looks at me as if I will know the answer.

'Er … well … I suppose it depends on whether you class the relationship as healthy, equal and consenting, and it isn't reinforcing your sexual interest in children. Sounds like there may be quite a bit to think about here – complicated stuff – and I'm not sure there is an easy answer.'

I do not think there are easy answers to any of this.

'So, Becky, that's them all sorted on the relationships front. What are we going to do about yours?' says Kenny in the debrief.

'Oh, I don't know. He's driving me mad. It's so up and down. He's jealous and possessive and controlling. He makes threats to leave, to kill himself – it's never-ending. We are both unfaithful.'

'Sounds like you need to do the relationships block!'

'I know, terrible, isn't it? Here I am lecturing them on healthy relationships, and I can't even have one myself. Talk about two-faced. I've got the same schemas as half of them and the most dysfunctional attachment style. It's me that needs to be in therapy.'

'None of us is perfect, Bec. It's what you do about it now that makes you different to them.'

'I know. I've got to end it, haven't I? I didn't realise he was so messed up. I think maybe the job gets to him as well. He can't drive past a lone woman without checking she is OK. And he worries he'll get wrongly accused of rape or murder or something and be arrested. He dreams about it – we are a right pair with our "murderer dreams", as we call them. Daniel just can't do relationships, though. I've tried to save him, and I can't. I need to save myself.'

I tell Daniel that night when he comes over after his evening shift. His eyes do that deepening, darkening thing and his lips go ever so white and tight.

'Well, on your head be it then. I've told you how my uncle put his head in the oven. You know I've got the same insurance policy.'

He delivers his killer line and storms out. I have cried it all out already and, despite the threat of suicide again, I feel lighter somehow, and relieved and determined. I have bought and not long moved into my very own cosy little terraced house. I have a lovely new tabby cat, a worthy career and good friends. I am going to be OK. And I hope Daniel will be too.

* * *

A couple of weeks later, as the sex and relationships block draws to an end, the three-legged rescue cat (I do like to rescue: car-mangled felines, damaged men, the list goes on) and I are snuggled up and purring on our IKEA sofa. I'm in my pyjamas, the gas fire is glowing, the curtains are drawn tight, and I've got a book in hand when the phone rings.

'Is that Rebecca Myers? It's HMP Graymoor. Will you come to the jail?'

It's not a question.

'Er, yes, why?' I say, shifting the warm, sleepy cat.

'Just come, please. Now. Immediately.'

CHAPTER TWENTY-FOUR

HOSTAGE

Driving down the dark, wet motorway in my trusty little car, my thoughts are running like they are competing for gold. *It must be my keys. I've taken them out of the prison and compromised the whole jail. They're calling me in to sack me. Maybe I let the keys out of my sight. Maybe several prisoners have escaped. And raped and murdered lots of people. Killed prison officers. The biggest prison escape in British history. Did I let the group see the keys? Did they take them when I wasn't looking? Have I become too friendly, become conditioned? They're calling me in to sack me and arrest me. I'll be put in a cell. It's all over. My career is done. I knew I did not deserve this career and I would fuck it up in the end.* I continue in this exhausting spiral until I have dropped Polly in the prison car park.

I approach the jail. It is about 8.30 p.m. I have never been there in the dark before and the gatehouse is empty. It feels so familiar, but at the same time as if there is no one at home – although hopefully all 800 of them are. I have not taken my keys home by mistake, have not taken them out of the jail – I checked the instant I put the phone down – but I cannot think of another reason why they would call me in at night. It feels strange being there in my jeans. And I have no bra or make-up on and my pyjama top underneath my hoodie. Two police cars are parked outside the gate. There is something wrong. *What the hell have I done?* I do not recognise the prison officer who meets me at the staff gate.

'Rebecca Myers, psychologist,' I say, holding my breath like a free-diver. 'Someone rang and asked me to come in straight away.'

The officer looks at me. His face is pale and under the fluorescent lights his eyes and sockets are dark. He reminds me of a panda.

'There's a hostage situation. The Governor's set up Silver Command [the Gold/Silver/Bronze Command structure was used in these situations. The Silver Commander is in tactical command on site, implementing the strategic directions passed down from the Gold Commander off site at Prison Service HQ] in the ECR [Emergency Control Room]. He wants a psychologist in with him. I'll take you up.'

I breathe out, coming up for air. *A hostage, for Christ's sake! So it isn't my bloody keys. And they need a psychologist. And they have me. Picked me? Why not one of the other, more experienced ones like Louise or Alex?* I feel a surge of relief. Then utter terror. I know that the prison service runs hostage negotiator training, but I haven't been on it yet. And at this point I have no idea what Silver Command is and hope someone will tell me, and soon. Adrenalin courses through me like I am strapped in and about to ride a huge roller-coaster. I hate roller-coasters, but a little bit of me feels a tingling anticipation. There is a fine line between fear and excitement. I want the challenge, yet I do not. I want to get off, but I do not. My skin and hair prickle and I suddenly feel more alive. More focused than perhaps ever before in my life.

Upstairs in Silver Command there are a few distressed men. And Alex Bull in her jeans and trainers. She is manic. Talking like she is on amphetamine and more than ready for the action.

'Hi, Rebecca,' she says. 'I'm heading down to see Bronze [the first person on the scene, who remains on the scene and becomes Bronze Commander, receiving and implementing instructions from Silver Commander]. I will take things from there. You stay here and advise Silver, the Number One. They want a psychological profile. Silver has got Gold on the line.'

The Number One Governor (the man in charge of the jail) considers me. He is a thin, permanently cross-looking man with a balding head and wispy side hair. He has a red, bulbous, pock-marked nose and hands that look like he has been standing out in a snowstorm for too long. He does not know who I am. I tell him I am a psychologist.

'What do you need for a profile?' he barks, phone in one hand, a communication wire sprouting out of his fleshy ear.

He looks like he is negotiating the Russian–American nuclear crisis.

There is another lower-ranking governor with him. A plumper, middle-aged, approachable man who is undoubtedly a great dad and husband. He should be at home right that minute putting his kids to bed and settling down with a cup of tea in front of the TV. He gives me a warm yet worried smile through his bushy ginger moustache. I am so pleased to see him. We know each other, this governor and me. We work on the wings together and on Sentence Planning Boards. My inner psychologist flickers into life. I can do this. I have to do this.

The Friendly-dad Governor tells me that at lock-up one of the prisoners called a female prison officer over to his cell. He wanted to ask her a question about the SOTP. I know her. She is a gentle, caring soul. He grabbed her and banged them up in his cell. She is in there now. Trapped and alone with him behind a heavy steel door. There is a weapon. Some sort of craft knife that he has for making the popular-only-in-prison matchstick models. The first officer on the scene is also someone I know well, and a very good friend of the female hostage. They are both SOTP colleagues. Decent, kind-hearted people doing their jobs and trying to help rehabilitate these damaged and dangerous men.

A wire has been set up outside the cell that transmits back to us in ECR. Bronze is there outside the cell door, talking to the perpetrator, and we can hear Bronze's deep voice echoing into the ECR like a badly tuned radio. Alex Bull is striding towards him and is going to advise from there. A specially trained team is being assembled from outside the jail somewhere. Our own Tornado (trained for emergency situations) prison officers are standing by outside the cell door. It will take time to remove the strengthened door. A minute or so at the very least. It will be noisy and will give the perpetrator time to harm, assault or kill the hostage if he wants to. Taking off the door, therefore, is the last option. We are going to try to negotiate him out.

Gold Command in Prison Service Headquarters, London, who are ultimately in charge, are advising down the phone line and relaying information to Silver.

'We need a code word,' says the Number One. 'Something I call if we have to take the door off. It will only be called in a matter of life or death. The code word will be "Green Custard". No one will say this by accident. Does everyone understand that the code word is Green Custard?'

I stand there. I am not sure of my place in this busy and agitated room. I have no official hostage negotiator training, but I know how to relate to prison staff at all levels. And I know sex offenders. I request the psychology files, SOTP files and prison records to build my profile. The Number One asks me if I need the IMR (Inmate Medical Record).

'That might be helpful, Sir, but ethically we have to have the inmate's permission for that.'

'Fetch the IMR!' snaps the Number One to one of the uniformed officers standing by in the room. The officer looks so young, like he is dressed up in his dad's clothes. He speeds off to the prison hospital without a word.

I borrow a pen and build my handwritten profile on a couple of sides of A4 taken out of the ECR printer. I am unsure about what a 'profile' looks like. I have never done one, and so I rely on my experience. What is the index offence? The pattern of offending? What might his risk factors be? What might the build-up to a new offence be? What do the negotiators need to know? *Will this even be any use in getting her out of there?*

The hostage-taker is already serving a life sentence. He is a serial rapist of elderly women in their own homes. His crimes have built up over time in severity, as is fairly often observed in sexual offenders. According to the hastily obtained IMR, he is a paranoid schizophrenic. I am a psychologist, not a psychiatrist, so although I include this in my 'profile', I am unsure as to how it might feed into his behaviour. I feel like I should know. I need to read some medical textbooks the minute I get out of here. He has been putting various applications in to the Psychology team, including one that very day, to see a psychologist about the SOTP. Chances are, given our demographics, he would have got a sole young female – me or Bronwyn perhaps. Was this a ploy? Had the hostage-taking been planned? Probably, I think. He is a Cat A, but absent on the 'not to be seen by a lone female' list. One of us would have gone on our own, as we do to see every serial rapist who puts in an app about SOTP. At a previous prison he tried to take another female prison officer hostage, but luckily she escaped.

There is evidence from his behaviour in previous offences that he is a sadist. There is some indication that he has psychopathic traits – callous, manipulative, criminally versatile – but he has not had a PCL-R. Wouldn't anyone who has taken an innocent person hostage and locked them in a cell be seen as callous and manipulative? My worry is that if he has strong psychopathic traits, this means we cannot appeal to his 'better nature'. We will struggle to encourage him to see the distress he is causing in the hostage, because he will not understand or care. Indeed, if he is a sadist, he may be enjoying it. We cannot use empathy for the hostage as a tool to get her out. Dr Hare and Mr Slade pop into my head. If he is highly psychopathic, we will need to play to what matters to him most: his status, his goals and his needs.

This is the gist of my profile: we have a forty-year-old sadistic, possibly psychopathic, paranoid schizophrenic who is a convicted serial rapist with a long history of criminal behaviour and sexual violence. His lengthy list of previous convictions indicates that punishment has no impact on his behaviour, that he will continue to act on his deviant sexual urges and that he has no concern for the consequences of his behaviour. He possibly prefers older women, maybe because they are more vulnerable or perhaps because that is his sexual preference. He has a history of hostage-taking. He is a planner, and this siege is probably premeditated. He has a weapon, and he is very capable of using it. Early stages of any assault on our hostage may be an indication that he is building up to something more severe. Given his sadistic/psychopathic tendencies, he will try to cause as much distress, terror and fear in the hostage as he can. He may threaten and torment and mock her. Threats should be seen as genuine. It is unlikely that appealing to his morality will be successful. He will not care about the distress of the victim; in fact, he will enjoy it and will be seeking it. He needs to be taken seriously and is capable of rape and, I hypothesise, murder. He is currently backed into a corner, has a life sentence anyway and therefore has nothing to lose. He may want to go out in glory.

I show it to the Number One, who grimaces.

The siege goes on all night. The hours are sluggish. He makes various demands: a helicopter to get out of the jail, money and freedom. These are all relayed through Bronze, up to Silver and then on to Gold in HQ. Of course, none of them are met. Bronze is calm throughout. I can hear his reassuring tone, talking to the hostage and to the prisoner through the door. Alex Bull is there, advising him. A specialist team is brought in, but the Number One remains in control and retains his own staff around him. He keeps calm and carries on, and I trust him.

And I do my best. I rely on myself and my knowledge and all the things I have learnt since that first over-whelming day when I stepped into the Centre. The team in the ECR is an unusual collection of people. Not selected. Not specially trained. In fact, none of us, to my knowledge, is trained at all in hostage negotiation. Most of the team just happened to be in the jail at the time, about to go off shift. I wonder how I made it here. Maybe people were called in because they appeared, alphabeti-cally, towards the top of the staff phone list. But my surname starts with an M. I have no idea how or why I was selected. Yet, we become a solid little team in those slow twelve hours. And they all treat me like an expert, with equality and respect. All the years of side-glances, the blatant ignoring, the message that young women are not fit for purpose in this environment fade away for that one night.

There is a lot of anxious waiting. Back and forth discussions with the prisoner play through the door, up the wire and into our room and are communicated to Gold Commander in London. The Number One asks for my advice. How should we play it? How should we answer the hostage taker and his demands? I have no one to ask.

So I use what I have learnt from the men in the groups. I know what worked with these men and what did not, usually anyway. And if I got it wrong and one of them flared up, I could calm him down. Or Kenny or Daniel could. But now I am on my own. I know we cannot afford to antagonise this man. I know he is very dangerous, and it could end in disaster. It will take a minute or so to get through the cell door and that may be too long to save her life. But I do not think he is the type we can talk out. I think he will rape or kill her or both. I know we will hear this down the line if he does. I can picture her soft, kind face in my mind. This is different to being in the group. I did not know those victims. I know this one. Rape and murder have always been second-hand, and I do not want to witness it for real. I want her out. We are on constant alert and the Number One cannot sit down. He wears a furrow in the carpet tiles with his pacing as we all, on both sides of the metal door, endure a long and agonising night.

The sky outside is a fuzzy grey again when suddenly there is a commotion down the line. We can all hear the beginning of an assault playing out into the hushed room. I hear things that will never leave my brain. Noises that I feel in my stomach before they reach my ears.

The Number One looks at me.

At me.

I meet his eyes and nod. We need to get her out of there. This is only going one way. It is now life or death. He calls it.

'GREEN CUSTARD! GREEN CUSTARD! GREEN CUSTARD!'

CHAPTER TWENTY-FIVE

A SHIFT INSIDE

Piped through in black and white on a CCTV camera, the Number One, Friendly-dad Governor and the rest of our bedraggled little night team watch the man who has caused so much distress walk down the main drag. Escorted by several officers, he is dressed in a white-paper evidence suit and they are heading for the Segregation Block. The police are there. He is a pathetic figure and I have a passing feeling of absolute hatred and disgust for this bastard of a man. I do not usually experience this with prisoners, whatever their crimes, but I have heard with my own ears what he has put our hostage through. I know that she, and perhaps the rest of us, will not recover from that slow and uncertain night. I cannot see our hostage – will never see her again – but she is physically safe at least. We got her out alive.

It is 8.30 in the morning and we emerge from the ECR like soldiers out of a trench. I gaze round at my incredible colleagues. After a night of no sleep, drinking bad coffee under fluorescent lights and trying to save a colleague's life, we look like we have been at war. Friendly-dad Governor looks as exhausted as a battle-field nurse. Alex Bull and I resemble walking casualties and look as if we need bandages round our worn-out heads. I still have my pyjama top on.

The Number One, our frontline general, is still attending to duty, and he calls a briefing of all the staff in the Visits Hall. The jail has opened up as normal, of course, and the officers have arrived for their shifts. There is a general sense of confusion as the siege has been on the local and national news. Rumours are rampant about who the hostage and perpetrator are. The little team from the ECR bustle into the hall and are invited to sit on the reserved front row, like we are the most important guests at a wedding or funeral. The Number One explains what has happened overnight without going into grim detail. I sit next to Alex, shaking like an anxious puppy. I feel cold to the bone and am worried my uncontrollable chattering teeth will distract the Number One. He thanks us all for our service and I feel so proud, yet also like I want to cry. We did it. We got her out. Yet somehow it does not feel like a triumph. The other psychologists crowd round after his talk. What happened? Are we OK? I can see Alex waving her arms around like an air-traffic controller, giving all to her story. The younger staff soak up every dramatic word. I have no make-up on. This is the first time I have ever been in the jail without mascara on. At that moment it is all I can focus on. All that has happened is already somewhat cut off.

I head out to my car. I am jittery and tingling with the after-effects of the adrenalin, yet weary and hollow. I feel as if someone has scooped out my insides. Part of me does not want to leave the jail. There is a lonely bed at home. I have no one to talk to. I am not in a relationship. I cannot and will not phone Daniel. I feel very alone in the world. Only my colleagues understand what I am feeling. No one else ever can or ever will. It is too unique. I am sent off duty and drive home to my cold, empty bed where I collapse and sob into my pillow. I wait for sleep. Disturbing images and sounds crash like rolling waves across my brain as the loyal disabled cat curls up, as ever, at my feet.

I am drawn back to the jail later that day, underwear on and make-up reapplied. I need to be with my colleagues. It is well known that a prison is a village, not a city, and the locals are gossiping. The staff are shocked and talking about what a good officer the hostage was. They retell the bits of the story they know. The sense of camaraderie in the jail is dialled up even further. Word has spread that I was in the ECR and I get 'You all right, love?' from several officers who normally ignore me. Although life in the jail rolls on, the incident is a blunt reminder that it could have been any of us. The prison is full of dangerous men, and it is easy to forget that sometimes when you get to know them.

I go into the group that afternoon. I walk in, see them all sitting expectantly in their usual seats, and their crimes strike me once again: they are all murderers, rapists and paedophiles. I have known that all along but have started seeing them as people. I have got to know their characters and personalities. Enjoyed their humour. Realised they are not all bad. What they have done has faded a little over time and, I admit it, I have grown to like them. I have spent more time with them in the last six months than I have with anyone else other than Kenny. I feel more cautious of them that day, bruised by what I have seen, heard and experienced. I feel a fresh, sore anger at them for what they have put their victims through.

'I knew that officer, she was lovely. She was bostin',' says Frank. 'She don't deserve that.'

'S'no worse than what we have done,' says Wayne.

'No, suppose not, but I *knew* her,' says Frank.

'Why does that make it different?' snaps Kenny.

'My victim wasn't real at the time; I didn't even know her name. She is now mind – real – all this group stuff has made it real.'

They talk about how angry they are with the hostage-taker and how the female officer might be feeling. This helps. They do not know it, but I need to see that I haven't got them all wrong. That people can change. That there is some hope in this godforsaken job.

The next week is tough. I can't begin to imagine what it is like for our rescued hostage. I keep running it over in my mind and hearing the raw noises from the cell coming down the wire. They ambush my thoughts when I am not expecting it. GREEN CUSTARD! GREEN CUSTARD! Should we have gone in sooner? Was my formulation right? How do you write a profile? Could I have done something differently, better, quicker? I am also filled with relief that she is physically safe, and that I held my own in that situation. I was the only woman in the ECR that night. *The only psychologist*. I did OK. We saved someone's life, and I was a part of it. I found strength in myself from somewhere and behaved like a bona fide forensic psychologist. My inner psychologist came alive and flourished exactly when I needed her. I hadn't even had the negotiator training. I had trusted in my experience and in myself. I do not need a man. I do not need Daniel or anyone to make it OK. My own belief in me is enough for now, and for once it feels good. A little warm glow burns underneath the other horror that surrounds the incident and keeps me going. I decide to apply for The Job. Maybe I am good enough after all.

* * *

'Every pan has its lid, Miss,' says Wayne. 'The main thing is, NO MORE VICTIMS.'

It is the last session of the group, and we are talking about what the men want from their futures. Wayne is hoping that he might have another girlfriend one day – find his lid. Out of all of them, I think he has travelled the furthest. I hope that he will make it in life, if and when the Parole Board see fit to release him. Will society ever trust him again? Will he get another chance before he dies? Despite the terror and destruction he has inflicted, I want him to have the opportunity to be free and make a life for himself. The shame and the label and the life sentence will be with him forever, helping him not to do it again.

I feel less confident about Sid. I cannot be sure that he hasn't conned us. There is a slippery aura about him, as if he is covered in a faint layer of grease and is a bit too slick to pin down. He is a master at manipulating people and excellent at keeping secrets. This is one of his schemas and it enabled him to offend for all those years. All that 'pal' business is part of the manipulation and grooming. I also know that his sexual preference is still for young boys. A sexual preference for children is the strongest predictor of sexual recidivism (reoffending). Those who offend against boys outside of the family (non-familial) are more likely to reoffend than those whose victims were girls or familial. His drive to offend is so strong that he has overcome the deterrent effect of punishment and prison many times. His sexual interest in young boys is fixed. I think that changing it would be like asking a straight man to be gay, as Kenny has suggested. Sid is now telling us that he wants to be in a relationship with a man nearer his own age, who looks young, but all the reports from the wing are that he hangs around with the younger, more vulnerable prisoners. He helps them out with tobacco and canteen, takes new arrivals under his wing as part of his role in the Listener scheme and then into his cell for illicit sex – essentially grooming them like he did his victims. He understands all the theory that Albany and we have taught him. He has filled in his schema diaries and been a good third facilitator. But we are not convinced. 'Everything before the but is bullshit' I hear the professor saying in my head. The behaviour from the wing is too worrying. It is offence-paralleling: a replica of how he groomed his victims. Thankfully he has a life sentence this time.

Despite our rocky start, Jeremy and I have reached some level of mutual respect along the way. He can still push my buttons and cause my imposter syndrome to flare like a firework, yet I am learning to understand that his narcissistic, superior exterior is concealing something softer. His apparent self-esteem is high, yet shaky underneath. He has worked hard on understanding why he offended and is pleased to have some answers. Convicted of murder and rape, I know he will be in prison for a long time. However, I think his offence is probably a catastrophic one-off. A complex set of circumstances, unlikely to be repeated, which led to the (im)perfect storm. He will always be prickly and socially awkward and find relationships and emotions tricky. That is part of his personality. However, I do not think he will rape or murder again. I can see him living outside of prison as an old man, reading his history books, visiting museums and following the rules of his life licence to the letter. He will probably get them laminated.

I feel like I know Colin the least. Hidden behind the ex-teacher persona, reading glasses and tidy beard lurks a man whose behaviour has been cruel and sadistic for many years. I do not warm to him, yet I can see that he is intelligent, and he has benefited from the programme. Statistically he is low risk – one intra-familiar female victim and no other convictions. I am just not sure that we have quite got to the truth of his sadism and deviant fantasy. The judge had the foresight to give him a life sentence due to the extremity of his crimes. I agree with his prescience.

Frank is one of the first prisoners I ever met while doing my early SOTP assessments. Despite him being a sexual murderer who so callously buried his victim in the garden, I have grown to like him as a person and even to enjoy his company. He is a man with many faults and difficulties and one who has committed a dreadful crime; nevertheless, he is a person all the same. He regrets his actions and has been so keen to learn from the group. Frank turned up clean-shaven to the group today – gone is the grisly black beard. There is another man emerging from underneath. Hopefully a straightening up on the outside is a representation of what is going on inside. I hope that he will go on to live a meaningful and offence-free life.

Nigel is still a bedraggled, smelly old child murderer. He has freely admitted a sexual interest in young school-girls. He will always present a risk, and I think it will be a very long time before he is ever released from prison. However, I admire him for his honesty. It must have been tough for him to sit in the group and open up in front of strangers about the biggest taboo and arguably the worst crime in society. His opinion of himself is crip-plingly low and he is going to need to work hard to overcome his view that there is something wrong with him. Maybe there is. Maybe a man who does this to a child cannot change and is forever deviant. Nonetheless, we work with all these men using the mantra that people can and do change if they want to. I truly believe the concept, and honour it with the vast majority of the pris-oners, most of the time.

I have been on my own journey alongside the men. I have learnt about my own interfering schemas and dysfunctional attachment style, and I have finally ended my destructive relationship. I have started to believe in my own abilities as a psychologist and grown as a facilitator in being able to work with live and presenting issues. As tough as the group has been, I have thrived on the challenge of working with these difficult men and have not been afraid to have demanding, probing and embarrassing conversations. However, like the men, I still have my issues: struggling with criticism, self-confidence and the ability to forgive. I am trying not to be an ice queen in my brand-new relationship, but it is tricky. 'No one messes with me' is always skulking in the shadows like a vampire, waiting for the opportunity to strike. The men have taught me that I am a work in progress just like them.

They all file out for the last time in a blur of stripes and denim, distinct prison odour and damp handshakes. I will miss them and the extraordinary bond we have created. The victims have not physically been with us for the last nine months, but they were always there in the background. Victims are the reason we do the work; saving future victims is the sole purpose of us all being in that fetid, intense room. I have heard details about the victims and the ghastly crimes against them that I know I will never repeat. They are private. The men trusted me with them, and I will always respect them and the victims with my discretion. As I sit there, I hope that the work we have done in the group will go some way to starting a process of transformation and ultimately preventing further victims. It will be my last group for a little while. I have been offered The Job.

CHAPTER TWENTY-SIX

ABOUT TWENTY
YEARS LATER

'The main sex offender treatment programme for England and Wales has been scrapped after a report found it led to more reoffending' announces one of the headlines of BBC News on 30 June 2017.

Articles follow in the *Guardian* and claims of making monsters worse are splattered across tabloids. The newspapers are reporting on the Ministry of Justice (MOJ) research that examined the sexual reconviction rate of 2,562 men who had started the Core SOTP between 2000 and 2012. The researchers matched the men in the study with a similar group of convicted sex offenders who had not taken part in the Core SOTP. They followed all the men into the community, some of them for almost fourteen years, some for less time, although the average was around eight years. The overall sexual reoffending rate for the Core SOTP offenders was 10 per cent and for the comparison group it was 8 per cent. When looking just at the reconviction rate for child images (child pornography) it was 4.4 per cent for the treated offenders and 2.9 per cent for the comparison group.

My first reaction is one of utter shock. An earlier evaluation, prior to the substantial roll-out of the SOTP across the prison estate, had appeared to show that attending the SOTP reduced the risk of reoffending in medium-risk men. Although the new research does not include the particular groups that I ran in the 1990s and have described here, I have invested more than a decade of my life in sex-offender treatment. I have seen for myself the individual changes in men like Frank, Wayne, even Jeremy, and have treated many more men since. I have witnessed them opening up about their innermost secrets, detected a change in self-confidence and an increase in their ability to relate to others. I have seen the sheer relief on their faces as they 'got' some of the reasons why their offending happened. I've encouraged them as they acknowledged faulty and unhelpful thinking, sexual interests and behaviours. Observed them practise new skills and learn strategies for managing themselves and their emotions. Noticed as they shaved off protective beards, lost weight, tidied their hair and took pride in their appearance. We enabled human connections in those groups. Some days I thought that it didn't matter who said what or how; it was enough for the men, just being in a supportive environment and having other humans take an interest in them. I thought we had given them the tools to help with challenges in the future. Of course, there were the men along the way who did not, would not or could not engage, and I know there is no absolute cure, whatever treatment is offered. I believe that we helped some men develop the means and motivation not to do it again. Could we really have made them worse?

The team at Headquarters responsible for the Core SOTP responds to the research with the following points:

- Some of the areas that the two groups are not matched on are potentially very relevant, including denial, attitudes, refusing the Core SOTP and deviant sexual interest (the strongest predictor of recidivism). As such, there may have been key differences between the two groups that impacted on the results (i.e. the Core SOTP treated group *were more deviant to start with*).

- The higher rate in the Core SOTP treated group is almost entirely child images reoffending. There is no difference between the two groups on serious adult or child *contact* offending. Can Core SOTP treatment represent a reduction in serious harm for the potentially more deviant men? In other words, did the treated men go from 'hands-on' to 'hands-off' offending?

- It is not an evaluation of the Extended SOTP and so no conclusions should be drawn about the

effectiveness of that programme (i.e. this
programme was not discredited).

I also know from personal experience that the nature
and, I believe, quality of the treatment was diluted somewhat in later groups. There was an overwhelming
pressure for SOTP treatment managers to 'get bums on
seats' and meet key performance indicators, bringing in
much-needed money to run the jails. So many groups
were running across the country, it was impossible to
have a psychologist involved in each one. Instead of carefully assessing the suitability and readiness of men for
the programme, treatment managers ran out of high-
risk sex offenders on the waiting lists. 'Scraping the
bottom of the barrel' was how I heard the composition of
one of the later SOTPs described. Putting lower-risk,
unsuitable men onto hamster-wheel programmes with
brand-new staff and not consistently providing psychological input or supervision ultimately impacted on
treatment integrity, in my view. This was in spite of the
mammoth attempts by those at Headquarters (including
me) to maintain overall quality in the face of ever-
increasing targets.

The result is that all sex-offender treatment programmes
in prisons in England and Wales are stopped immediately. Some men are partway through groups, and this
must be very confusing and challenging for them and

their facilitators. The response to the research by the staff involved over the years is one of immense disappointment and upset. Elizabeth displays immeasurable humility and resilience, and true to her steadfast belief in evidence-based practice she leads the way in accepting the research findings and learning from them. As she says, it does not work out as we hoped it would, but all is far from lost.

Fortunately, the evolution of the SOTP is already well established. The team at Headquarters responsible for sex-offender treatment have always run their own internationally respected research programme. When the headlines break, preparations are already under way for an overhaul of the suite of SOTPs to bring them in line with the most recent in-house evidence and global scientific developments. The news brings the introduction of the enhanced programmes forward.

Like a phoenix rising from the flames, a new generation of treatment programmes is now delivered across the prison estate. Strength-based, and like the Core and Extended SOTPs before them, they rely on the latest international research. Careful and consistent evaluation to the very highest standards will be crucial and ethically non-negotiable. In addition to new groupwork programmes, named Horizon and Kaizen (from the Japanese, meaning 'continuous improvement'), there is an individualised module called the Healthy Sex Programme. Delivered by a psychologist, this work focuses on exploring exactly what it says on the tin, in addition to teaching skills for healthy relationships. And alongside this, there is a Medication to Manage Sexual Arousal initiative, in which doctors or psychiatrists can prescribe – usually anti-depressant – medication (which lacks the unpleasant side-effects of hormone treatments) to help reduce sexual desire/preoccupation in those volunteers who are assessed as being suitable.

On Horizon and Kaizen, the offenders do not even have to admit to their offences; they can do the treatment and maintain their innocence. The thinking is that if relevant risk factors are identified and worked on, behind the scenes if you like, this will still impact on behaviour. Impulse control, poor coping and relationship skills, or unhelpful attitudes about women, children and sex can be addressed without details of how they featured in any particular offence. There is also growing evidence that denial and shame can be protective factors and reduce the risk of future reoffending, particularly in high-risk offenders. One hypothesis is that these factors can help to hold self-esteem intact, in turn reducing the risk.

I like this approach. When I think about the shame that Wayne held onto, and the childhood abuse we raked through, I feel that this may have been a better method for him and the many others like him who had backgrounds scattered with trauma.

Giving an offence account and confrontation over specific 'facts' of the offending no longer happens – there is none of Max's 'throwing the deps' at anyone. One of the critiques of the Core SOTP was that there was too much focus on the offence stories without any basis in the evidence that this reduces offending. I look back with reticence at the dogged pursuit, the picking and the challenging that we put some of the men through in the 'hot seat' and I can see why they dreaded it. It was always done with the best intentions, yet if you treat people with kindness and respect when exploring their past, it fits that you might get a better result. And how just knowing the precise details of what happened was going to stop anyone from doing it again, I was never clear.

The victim empathy blocks of the treatment were also abandoned due to lack of evidence of effectiveness (the re-enactments had gone before 2000 when the research started). My own experience of the re-enactment role plays was that they felt like putting your hand in a nest of biting spiders. Why on earth would you want to do it, given the possible consequences? Playing the role of a victim being sexually assaulted was difficult for those who had been sexually abused and, overall, a shaming experience for the men. And then there is the issue of men taking part or watching it and becoming aroused, as I suspected Kyle did all those years ago. Another concern of the research was that by focusing on exactly what happened in the offences, the offenders were leading each other to be more deviant by taking on each other's faulty thinking and behaviour. So, while these

blocks of treatment *felt* right to many treatment staff –
and, it should be noted, often the prisoners themselves
– there is no evidence that they worked.

Treatment has also become more holistic and individualised. Less of a one-size-fits-all approach. The role of
different learning styles, cognitive impairments, mental
illness and personality disorders and traits are far better
understood and are included in formulation (a collabo-
rative hypothesis of how and why the offending
happened and in some cases was maintained) and treatment planning. It is acknowledged that group work is
not everything: other pathways such as employment,
training and education are also vitally important in
reducing risk. We know about the value of social capital,
hope, agency and the creation of a new desisting identity
(a prosocial/non-criminal personal identity) that is at
odds with an offending identity. I think about Jeremy
when I read this research. He never did see himself as a
criminal.

The world is changing too. In the 1990s and early 2000s
we delivered treatment in a sexist, racist, homophobic,
male-dominated prison environment, but also within a
toxic society that condoned and propagated deeply
entrenched misogyny and inequality; against a backdrop
of an internet countdown on the hours until the under-
age chorister Charlotte Church could lose her virginity
(I struggled for a response to the confused child sex

offender who showed me the newspaper reporting on this); alongside the overt sexualisation of a young Britney Spears in school uniform – so admired by Nigel – with the lyrics 'Hit me, baby, one more time' apparently, at least, barely concealing a reference to domestic violence; beside frequent 'slut-shaming' (what a term) and victim-blaming, including by judges in rape cases. While there are still (too) many examples of inequality and sexual harassment, thanks to international movements like 'MeToo' we at least have a lexicon for it now. We didn't at the time; we were desperate, lone voices finding our way.

We know that sexual abusers are film producers, TV stars, celebrities and political figures, but also police officers, husbands and the man next door. They are not just monsters stalking the streets at night grabbing strangers to rape and murder, which thankfully remains rare (although whatever we do, I think unfortunately there will always be the odd unstoppable psychopath). We also have the Independent Inquiry into Child Sexual Abuse, despite its false starts and criticism, trying to unearth, expose and understand the ingrained cultures that concealed and perpetuated sexual violence to children within institutions in the UK.

Treatment is therefore set against a somewhat different context these days, and this can only be helpful. The majority of people know it is not OK to call women 'birds' or 'pussy', or to have a page-three calendar up in the office, even if you do cover the nipples with NSPCC stickers. And even if people *do* think that is OK, they wouldn't get away with it in most government workplaces these days.

The rehabilitative culture in prisons has creaked along too. There are many, many more psychologists in prisons, and they are mostly women. Some prisons have whole wings or specialist units dedicated to treatment, some of which are 'psychologically informed', with specially trained prison officers dedicated to the continued rehabilitation of offenders. The key-worker scheme, where each prisoner is paired with a prison officer, again recognises the importance of developing individual human relationships. I have personally witnessed this system yield incredible results in terms of engaging prickly, overlooked, long-term prisoners who are rotting in the system. The trauma-informed approach (where individual needs resulting from past or ongoing trauma are recognised) that is now used in women's prisons is yet to trickle into the way we deal with men, yet I am hopeful that one day it might.

The prison service is the forgotten service. Prison officers are not held up as superheroes in quite the same way as frontline staff in other public services. I know from my continued work in prisons that there are many excellent prison officers doing fantastic work in an incredibly tough and under-resourced environment. Prisons are not gushing with money. Jails are not seen as valuable recipients from the public purse – who wants their hard-earned taxes to pay for looking after the burden of those who have committed appalling crimes? Yet we want reformed prisoners. We can't have it both ways.

Like any branch of science, revolutionary ideas are introduced, tested and modified over time. *Hirudo medicinalis*, or medicinal leeches, were first used in Ancient Egypt by the doctors of emperors and have been widely used to treat disease, nervous disorders and even haemorrhoids. We now use different approaches to treat these concerns. However, the idea was revised and allowed to evolve, and leeching is still used in plastic and reconstructive surgery. Practitioner scientists with integrity carry out their research, then reflect and refine. They acknowledge mistakes and embrace evidence that suggests there may be a more effective way. Society should not blame, punish or belittle these attempts. Doing so will inhibit innovation and prevent progress.

And so, the work and its dedicated workers have carried on. This is what it is to be pushing a way forward in concepts we don't fully understand yet know we need to address. Society does not want or welcome sexual violence and child abuse, and rightly so. Incarcerated men who have committed sexual offences, especially against children, are seen as the scum of society and are held up as subhuman. My experience has taught me that underneath it all they are not so different from the rest of us.

However, I wouldn't want my compassionate view of the men as being (whatever is) normal, worthwhile and deserving of a second chance to be misinterpreted as sympathy or condoning their actions. It certainly is not. Yet if we can try to treat men who have committed sexual offences this way, then we stand a much better chance of success. *And so do they*. We know that vilifying, stigmatising and ostracising these men does not help. If we shun and isolate them, deny them jobs and a sense of purpose, then the paradox is that they are even *more* likely to offend. Essentially, it will take us all to help these men not to recidivate. Contrary to popular belief, the majority of men convicted of sexual offences desist (stop) naturally. In the 2017 MOJ research the overall sexual reoffending rate (excluding breach of licence/ community conditions) was 7.5 per cent, and this included high- and very high-risk men. Over 90 per cent of the men desisted, i.e. they did *not* reoffend.

We do not have the death penalty in the UK. Whole-life tariffs are rare. The serious reoffence rate of offenders released by the Parole Board, despite the bad press they receive, is impressive – less than 1 per cent. And the Parole Board are only involved in the most severe cases – those with long sentences. We do not lock people up and throw away the key, and consequently men who have committed sexual offences are released every day, some automatically, some on parole. Released sex offenders are subject to strict monitoring and controls, but inevitably they do have to live somewhere. At the very least, it will take a mindful tolerance of men who have previously committed sex offences for them to resettle. Successful, safe reintegration of ex-offenders into the community and a second chance for them to belong and contribute is the ultimate goal of all clinicians and criminal justice professionals. And for most of the men themselves, in my experience.

Your new neighbour might be someone who was neglected, sexually abused, mercilessly beaten and made to watch his mother being raped while he was tied to a radiator. And all before the age of ten years old, while his impressionable brain was still growing. Just like Wayne. I have absolutely no doubt you would have rescued him from such cruel horror as a young child if you could. Damaged children grow up. Now that child is an adult, can you find it in yourself to play a role in helping him live safely in our society? It is a question we *all* need to be asking ourselves, and with the bigger picture in mind: the prevention of sexual violence.

EPILOGUE

I wish I knew what happened to the men on my first SOTPs. This is a frustration of the job: I only get to hear the bad news and not the successes. After treatment, we typically had very little contact with the men. We carried on with the next group and they carried on with their sentences. I have an update on just a few of them.

Frank was released last year on parole. Within a week of release, he went to the pub and failed to return to the probation hostel where he had to spend the night. He therefore broke his life licence conditions and was returned to prison that same day. I was sad, annoyed and terribly disappointed in him. *How thoughtless can you be, Frank?* What a waste, after all that time inside. Maybe that's the point; he just could not cope after all that time in prison. It will take him a while to get out on parole again, if ever. At least he did not reoffend. You could argue that the damage done was only to himself.

Angry Kyle is still in prison and at least fifteen years over tariff. He will be in his forties now, hopefully slowing down and burning out from his violence, although he is likely still struggling with some aspects of his behaviour and enduring personality traits.

Andy made it right through to Category-D/open-prison conditions – a prison with less security (for example, no fence or wall), less supervision and a chance to have home visits and to work in the local community – but was returned to closed prison after breaking the rules and having a mobile phone in his cell.

I know that after almost forty years in prison in total, Sid also made it to open prison and was due for release. He was many years past his tariff but was held up for release by his admissions about his unhealthy interests in young boys. This is very unlikely to disappear over time, although age may have helped, and he will need to be managed carefully on release if that is what the Parole Board decides.

Short of tracking them down, I don't know about Jeremy, Wayne, Nigel and Colin. Serious reoffences involve a Serious Further Offence (SFO) review. An SFO is triggered when an offender is charged with a serious offence while on probation supervision or shortly after it ends. The reports are publicly available, and I have not seen one for any of the men. Nor have I seen them on the *News at Ten*, so no news is good news, I hope. They may all still be in prison.

Mr Slade is still inside too, unlikely ever to be free – thankfully so, I believe. Life, of course, does mean life unless you are considered to meet the test for release (although a life licence can be revoked at any time). I'm not sure he ever will. I do know he got married to a female pen pal and had a wedding in the prison chapel. I hear his suit was a sight to behold.

I am still healing from my childhood. I sometimes wonder if that's all we do as adults. Or maybe I have just met a disproportionate number of people who had a tough start. Forgiveness is not easy, but bitterness is worse, and my relationship with my mum is better than it has ever been. Holding onto the grievance and anger began to feel like someone was gripping my heart with an iron glove. I have to accept as part of my psychological training that humans have flaws, that people make mistakes, and in doing so they damage others. It's way harder to apply on a personal level. Letting some of it go, for the sake of myself, my children and my mum brings a sense of freedom that helps me live a happier life. I do believe that what happened to me has allowed me to do a job I love and do it well. It enabled me to be the person and psychologist I am, allowed me to shut off when I needed to and made me as tough as an old boot! I try to work on not letting yesterday take up too much of today as best I can.

I got my ice queen under control early enough to allow my new relationship – just developing after the hostage situation – to thrive. We are still happily married almost two decades later, although like any relationship there have been challenges. To borrow a quote from Wayne, 'every pan has its lid' and I found mine. Facilitating on the SOTP, particularly the Extended Programme, taught me so much about myself, my schemas and attachments. A valuable learning process for me as well as the men.

Daniel committed suicide just a few weeks after our wedding. Despite seeking professional help, in the end he could not cope with being himself, with relationships or with life. I don't think the job helped; he was tainted by the offences, the misogyny and the over-inflated masculine culture that he tried to keep up with – that men have to be strong and silent and have to treat women in a certain way. Arguably, he excelled at this behaviour, yet underneath he was needy and fragile. He questioned his maleness and the role of men in society: how male privilege and violence could be so easily used against women. He worried about being accused of a crime he did not commit and that, simply because of being a man, he would be dumped in the same sexual-predator category as the prisoners were. Daniel was an admired, approachable, well-respected prison officer. A strong and powerful advocate of programmes, treatment and the possibility of offender change, and was at his very best looking after the men on the wing and sorting out their problems.

So he used his insurance policy to opt out, just like he always told me he would. The news that he'd taken his own life rocked me to my core. It took some ten years before I was healed enough not to think about it every single day and rehearse what I could and should have done differently. I know that guilt is a wasted emotion, but (and everything before the but is bullshit) Professor Bunting's advice was hard to employ in this tragic situation, and still is, two decades on.

Sadly, dear Len died from alcoholism several years ago. He loved a pint, but it got to him in the end. He was always a heavy drinker. It went with the culture. Maybe he fell in deeper to cope with the work, maybe not. He never returned to sex-offender treatment.

And then there is the loss of Elizabeth. Such an incredible, dedicated woman who made understanding and tackling sexual violence her life's work. Who inspired so many others, including me, to do the same. Elizabeth lost her battle with cancer last year. Although I did not see her in the last couple of years, when she was ill, her early death had a cutting impact on me. From the moment I saw her in the training room, I wanted to be like her and to be liked by her. She was my mentor, teacher and advisor. My professional hero. Supervisor, boss and friend. And a good, generous, humble and incredibly intelligent human being. As an astute friend said, I wish I had told her those things while she was alive. Never seeking fame nor fortune, she remained with the prison service, working for the greater good of humanity as long as she was able. She was known, loved, admired and respected by staff, clinicians and academics at all levels right across the world. Prisoners liked her too and she enjoyed nothing more than talking to them about their rehabilitation and trying to do her best by them. She was a Goliath: strong, yet vulnerable. The world of sex-offender research and treatment is mourning and missing her. And so am I.

The loyal Kenny, who truly deserves a medal, is still at Graymoor, and is still doggedly trying to prevent future victims, as am I, Bronwyn and, last I heard, Alex Bull, although we work in different fields of forensic psychology now and all drifted away from Graymoor. It's a mind-breaking, soul-shattering, exhausting, frustrating, fascinating and rewarding job, and not one you can easily walk away from …

Let me describe an incident that happened just the other day. I am walking the dog down a country lane near my house and pass a hatchback car parked in a lay-by. The boot door is raised. A lone man is sitting on the edge of the boot drinking tea out of a Thermos. A long, slow shiver sweeps through me, like a cold wind has pierced my skin and is chilling my spine and internal organs. My thoughts turn over to the dead-eyed wannabe serial killer Mr Slade. My high-scoring psychopath. I cross the road and then come the racing, automatic thoughts. Is this strange man lying in wait to kidnap someone? Me? Is he a rapist or murderer? Why else would he be sitting there? I drop into potential rapist/murderer/kidnapper alert mode. I scan him and take a careful mental note of his features and clothes, just in case I later need to pick him out of a line-up. Then I have a wave of guilt: identifying him may mean someone has died. I can't help but notice a picnic blanket too, neatly rolled alongside what looks like a toolbox in the boot. *What is it with rapists and picnic blankets?* I take a note of the registration plate, although it is partly obscured by his long legs. I repeat it several times to the dog, trying to push it into my longer-term memory.

Then the passenger door swings open and I breathe out as a jolly round woman, dressed in walking clothes and hiking boots, emerges from the passenger seat. The would-be kidnapper pours her a cup of tea with a warm smile. She joins him on the boot edge, and they give each other a little 'Cheers!' with their plastic cups.

'Silly old me,' I say out loud to the understanding dog.

So, these are the things I live with. A fairly permanent suspiciousness schema and seeing potential kidnap, rape and child abuse in situations that are harmless. I am over-protective of my children, never more so than when they were younger. There was no chance of them ever camping in the garden overnight on their own or talking to the boiler man at the swimming baths. I panicked when they went into public toilets without me and I resisted male babysitters. I hate knives sticking upright out of butter or, worse still, out of meat. Cable ties give me the creeps, as do gorilla face masks, picnic baskets and rugs. The theme tune to *Coronation Street* occasionally makes me shudder and want to look behind the sofa. I've still got the brain tattoo of Frank's pale, lifeless, mud-spattered victim in her shallow garden grave, and several more inked on since.

Overall, though, the experience of working with these men was a positive one. There was a strong sense of achievement, camaraderie and joint purpose, and of making a difference and trying to change and build people's lives for the better. I'm probably a better parent as a result – more suspicious and protective, yes, but also able to discuss the issues of consent and respect, attitudes to women and sex openly with my teenage boys. It's *so* important. I've certainly made them more aware of the dangers of sexual abuse and of the importance of talking to us about their problems and relationships.

Ultimately, I am immensely proud of our dedication to the various research and treatment programmes and the continued evolving rehabilitation attempts over the years. It's not easy or comfortable work. If it was, everyone would be doing it. I also believe that somewhere there are men, women and children who are still alive, or have been saved from sexual abuse, because those of us who work in this often-misunderstood world give our everything, and gift a little, non-returnable piece of ourselves, to this grim and gritty work. It's a fair swap in my book.

ACKNOWLEDGEMENTS

Firstly, thank you to Andrew Lownie, my agent, for picking me out of his inbox and launching me into the publishing world with such professionalism and efficiency I could barely catch my breath.

Thank you to Ajda Vucicevic, my editor, for her boundless positivity and enthusiasm for the book, and her support of me whilst I navigated the joy/terror of becoming a first-time published author. Huge thanks and appreciation to the rest of the hardworking team at HarperCollins.

To The Literary Consultancy for providing the two talented and expert professional editors Frankie Bailey and Sue Lascelles, who shaped early drafts and gave me the push to contact the Andrew Lownie Literary Agency.

Thank you to my early readers Lisa, Dave and Michelle, and astute beta reader and advice-giver extraordinaire Jo. Also, to the best sounding board a person could ask for – both whilst writing a first book and negotiating life in general: Stephen. Not forgetting the fabulous women on the Jessica Lourey writing course in Paris, 2019, for giving me the inspiration and encouragement to give it all a go.

To my colleagues, past and present, for sharing their lives and keeping me standing. And, finally, to the many prisoners along the way. For trusting me with their stories.